WHAT **NOT** TO WRITE

ASPEN PUBLISHERS

WHAT **NOT** TO WRITE

Real Essays, Real Scores, Real Feedback

LawTutors
Massachusetts Bar Exam
Essay Book

Tania N. Shah, Esq.
President and Founder of LawTutors, LLC

Melissa A. Gill, Esq.
Head Attorney Instructor for LawTutors, LLC

Wolters Kluwer
Law & Business

AUSTIN   BOSTON   CHICAGO   NEW YORK   THE NETHERLANDS

ISBN 978-07355-7834-0

Library of Congress Cataloging-in-Publication Data

Shah, Tania N.
   What not to wirte: real essays, real scores, real feedback y / Tania N. Shah, Melissa A. Gill.
      p. cm.
   "LawTutors Massachusetts Bar Exam Essay Book."
   ISBN 978-0-7355-7834-0
   1. Bar examinations—Massachusetts—Study guides. 2. Law—Massachusetts—Examinations, questions, etc. 3. Legal composition—Study guides. I. Gill, Melissa A. II. Title.

KFM2476.s524 2008
340.076—dc22

                                                                    2008046190

About Wolters Kluwer Law & Business

Wolters Kluwer Law & Business is a leading provider of research information and workflow solutions in key specialty areas. The strengths of the individual brands of Aspen Publishers, CCH, Kluwer Law International and Loislaw are aligned within Wolters Kluwer Law & Business to provide comprehensive, in-depth solutions and expert-authored content for the legal, professional and education markets.

CCH was founded in 1913 and has served more than four generations of business professionals and their clients. The CCH products in the Wolters Kluwer Law & Business group are highly regarded electronic and print resources for legal, securities, antitrust and trade regulation, government contracting, banking, pension, payroll, employment and labor, and healthcare reimbursement and compliance professionals.

Aspen Publishers is a leading information provider for attorneys, business professionals and law students. Written by preeminent authorities, Aspen products offer analytical and practical information in a range of specialty practice areas from securities law and intellectual property to mergers and acquisitions and pension/benefits. Aspen's trusted legal education resources provide professors and students with high-quality, up-to-date and effective resources for successful instruction and study in all areas of the law.

Kluwer Law International supplies the global business community with comprehensive English-language international legal information. Legal practitioners, corporate counsel and business executives around the world rely on the Kluwer Law International journals, loose-leafs, books and electronic products for authoritative information in many areas of international legal practice.

Loislaw is a premier provider of digitized legal content to small law firm practitioners of various specializations. Loislaw provides attorneys with the ability to quickly and efficiently find the necessary legal information they need, when and where they need it, by facilitating access to primary law as well as state-specific law, records, forms and treatises.

Wolters Kluwer Law & Business, a unit of Wolters Kluwer, is headquartered in New York and Riverwoods, Illinois. Wolters Kluwer is a leading multinational publisher and information services company.

Dedication

This book is dedicated to all the future lawyers about to embark upon the bar exam. We know you can do it, now YOU need to know you can do it.

Acknowledgments

We would like to relay our deepest gratitude to all of our students who selflessly contributed their essays to this book so that other students could learn from them. Without you, your experience, your trust and your input, this book would not exist.

Contents

WHAT **NOT** TO WRITE

Introduction

WHAT **NOT** TO WRITE: MASSACHUSETTS

Dear Students,

We have to admit, here at LawTutors we *love* that show *What Not to Wear* on TLC and we wondered if we could relay the same message about bar exam essay writing that the producers of the show do about fashion. So, here it is, a tool to help you learn what NOT to write on the bar exam, as well as what TO write. We are also hoping we can be just as entertaining, but we will settle for your learning valuable skills and passing the exam!

WHAT THIS BOOK **IS**

This book is different than any other book on writing essays for the bar exam. First, we show you REAL essay answers: all essays in this book are questions from past bar exams, and the answers are actual essays written by bar candidates. Nothing within the actual essays has been changed; even grammar and spelling are kept intact. This gives you an idea of what "good" and "bad" essays look like through the eyes of the bar examiners. The only thing that has changed in between what they saw and what you are seeing is the handwriting. We understand that it may be helpful to see the actual handwriting of the exam taker under time pressure, but this is not practical for the purposes of a book. Also, have no fear, all of our students have given us permission to use their essays!

Second, this book shows you that you do not always need a perfect essay to gain a perfect score. Oftentimes, our students become overwhelmed by sample essays they see in commercial books; these samples are written by attorneys who use notes and may have an unlimited amount of time. Those samples are not only daunting, but also unobtainable on the actual day of the bar exam. What this book showcases *is* obtainable.

Because we want to show you obtainable answers, we will not be providing model answers. We believe that giving you model answers will not benefit you, as it would be impossible for you to replicate what we can write, with unlimited time and resources, in 36 minutes. Therefore, we will only be offering advice and suggestions.

Third, this book is a tool to practice your essays and then compare them to the "good" and "bad" answers. We have given you space to write your own critique, and it is to your benefit to think about what is good or bad, and make your own comments. We have found that this approach helps students learn how to write much more than asking leading questions to guide you through your comments. We want you to come to your comments on your own. Obviously, we cannot force you to utilize the space to write your own comments, but it really will help you learn how to write a better essay.

After you have thought about what YOU think, you can flip to what our comments are. These helpful hints tell you exactly why an essay received a good or bad score. Notice what is similar in the answers that earned 7s (the highest score possible), and contrast that with what is similar in the answers that earned 1s (the lowest score possible).

We realize that your comments might not mirror ours, and that's okay—the goal is to THINK about what makes the answers good and bad. In addition, we also realize that some comments might be redundant, but we hope that rather than have that frustrate you, it will help you see the similarities in all of the bad answers, and the similarities in all of the good answers, so that you may more easily replicate the good answers.

Fourth, we realize that in some cases, you may wonder why a certain essay got a low score and why a certain essay got a higher score, even though the same issues were spotted in both. This book will show you that two examinees may spot the same issues but organize them and express them in ways that make a crucial difference in scoring. This also brings us to the organization of the book. Some students like starting with the "1" essays and going up, building themselves to the "7" essays. Other students have told us they want to see the "7" essays first, and then have us end with the "1" essays. However you wish to go through the book is up to you. We have organized it from "7" answers in the beginning to "1" answers at the end. If you feel strongly about going through the essays in the reverse, you may start at the end of the book.

WHAT THIS BOOK IS **NOT**

This book is *not* like your other essay books.

Frankly, we believe there are a multitude of very helpful books out there on answering the call of the question, outlining your answer, and writing your essay. We believe that our introduction here is very helpful in tackling these issues, but it is not what our entire book is about. Let's admit it, if you haven't heard a ton of advice on how to write a good essay by now, you are definitely going to hear it during your bar review studies. There are tried and true published techniques, and we are not worried that you will not get enough exposure to these techniques. What we are worried about is that you will not have enough exposure to *actual written bar exam essays*. These speak for themselves, and no amount of technique can give you the type of lessons you learn from actual scored essays.

Hence, the focus of this book is not to teach you substantive law or writing the perfect essay *directly*. The focus of the book mirrors its title: what *not* to write, which is essentially about learning the good from the bad. At the end, you will also learn the good from the good.

We are not writing a book on essays by way of a "lecture" format but by way of an "example" format. This is also not a book on substantive law, because we are pretty sure you have one or two or ten of those. While we point out the rules of law, where applicable, in our discussion of the actual essays, we want the student to learn from some of our more general comments and apply them to a multitude of essays; once the student does this, he or she will be prepared to write on *any* essay.

Most of all, we do hope that in addition to learning how to write a great bar exam essay, you have some fun with this book. After all, we had fun writing it.

Sincerely,

Tania N. Shah, Esq.
President and Founder of LawTutors, LLC
www.lawtutors.net
tania.shah@lawtutors.net

Melissa A. Gill, Esq.
Head Attorney Instructor for LawTutors, LLC
melissa.gill@lawtutors.net

The Massachusetts Bar Exam

AN INTRODUCTION TO THE MASSACHUSETTS BAR EXAM

Since Massachusetts uses a combined Multistate-Essay score of 270 as its passing mark, a high Essay score will offset a lower Multistate score. For those of you who have a tough time scoring high on standardized tests, it is important that you perform your best on the essay portion with a high score.

We know it stresses you out to think about writing enough essays to cover *all* the subjects that may be tested on the day of the exam as well as all the possible sub-topics that may be tested on any one given subject. We suggest that you do a combination of writing, outlining, and reading essays for each subject that is tested so that you both practice your writing and outlining skills while maximizing your exposure to the "types" of essays tested within a subject.

FORMAT OF THE MASSACHUSETTS ESSAY EXAM

The Massachusetts Essay exam consists of ten questions based on a statement of facts, each calling for an essay answer. These essays are scored from 1 to 7, 7 being the best, and 1 being the worst. Ideally, you want to do the best you can on each essay, but a solid 5 across the board will leave you in a safe zone. The occasional 4 is nothing to worry about, but you still want to strive for 5s and 6s.

The examination is six hours long, with a three-hour morning session consisting of questions 1 through 5 and a three-hour afternoon session consisting of questions 6 through 10.

Each applicant must answer five questions in a three-hour period. This means that in the space of 36 minutes, an applicant must (a) read a fact pattern one or two typed pages long, and (b) construct a three- to four-page written answer to that question.

TESTED AREAS

You will be expected to be familiar with the law in the following fields:

Agency
Business Organizations
Civil Procedure
Constitutional Law
Contracts
Criminal Law
Descent and Distribution of Estates
Domestic Relations
Evidence Including the Federal Rules of Evidence
Massachusetts Procedure
Professional Responsibility
Real Property
Torts
Trusts
Uniform Commercial Code (Articles 1 through 9)
Wills
Federal Jurisdiction and Venue
Unfair and Deceptive Practices (G.L. c. 93A)

HOW IS THIS DIFFERENT FROM EVERY ESSAY YOU HAVE WRITTEN IN LAW SCHOOL?

You may be thinking that you know how to write essays, since you have been doing it for at least three years. But please note that these essays are MUCH different from what you have been writing for law school.

First and foremost, your professors were testing your knowledge of the law, so it was important to dazzle them with obscure nuances of the law that they taught you, and they were expecting you to argue both sides of the issue.

However, the bar examiners assume you know the law—after all, you graduated law school. The bar examiners want to see how you apply that law to the facts, so a more minimalist approach is necessary. Putting too much in the essay will not only take up too much of your time, which you do not have, but it will lead the bar examiners to think that you are unsure of yourself, and are going in directions that are unnecessary.

Again, unlike law school, where the goal was to test your knowledge of the law, the point of the bar exam is to test whether you have the skills to be a lawyer. This means getting straight to the point, and analyzing only what is relevant.

WRITING THE ESSAY EXAMINATION
PART OF THE MASSACHUSETTS BAR EXAM

1. *Sit on Your Hands:* We are all guilty of stabbing pen to margins as we read the fact pattern for the first time: today is the day to STOP doing that. Read the fact pattern first as a "story" so you can take everything in. If you start writing issues in the margins right away, you may think the fact pattern is going somewhere it is not, and you have just wasted precious time going down the wrong path. In addition, focus on the call of the question before you start outlining issues, and only answer what the question is asking. Under no circumstances (and we DO mean this) should you answer a question that is not there.

2. *The Outline:* Decide on a logical, orderly, and convincing arrangement for the statement of your views: Will it be party by party? Property by property? Chronological order? What arrangement makes the most sense in covering as many of the issues as possible, without being repetitive or disorganized? There is no right or wrong way to outline; it is merely a way to prepare to write an essay. Some students believe that this takes up valuable time, but the reality is that if you spend five minutes on an outline, your essay will be more coherent, and you will be less likely to miss important issues. In fact, you do not have time *not* to outline. Take time to brainstorm, or create a checklist. Not only will this make for a better-organized essay, but you are less likely to miss issues or end up getting overly excited about knowing a topic and spouting it all on the page.

   We have provided a few sample outlines throughout the book, but remember, the outline is only for you, and to help you prepare to write. Do not spend time stressing over mastering the "perfect" outline.

3. *The Fact Pattern Is Given to You: There Is No Need to Rewrite It:* We are going to draw from some advice from the people who matter: the Massachusetts Board of Bar Examiners. The examiners know what the facts are and you have no time to waste.[1] Do not set up a fact

---

1. *Massachusetts Board of Bar Overseers: Suggestions on Writing the Essay Examination.*

section, or spend valuable time and space restating what is already in the question. Remember, however, that the facts should be applied, as necessary, in the analysis. Remember, we told you that this was different from a law school essay, and that you want to be more succinct and minimalist. This is one more way to achieve that.

4. ***Do Not Throw in the Entire Hornbook on Contracts:*** Do not start your answer with a legal proposition; the rule of law comes later and can be combined into your analysis.[2] You also do not need to state the law in full intricate detail; simply make a sufficiently detailed reference to it so that the examiners do not have to wonder whether you know the law. As we stated before, unlike your law professors, the examiners are not interested in knowing how many rules of law you have learned, but rather want to know the way you apply the applicable rules to the facts stated. Keep in mind that unlike a law school exam, there is no need to throw in everything you know about a certain subject. Avoid sentences that start "However, if this had happened" or "If the facts had been different …". The bar examiners are giving you the facts they want you to use, so do not create new ones.

5. ***Discuss All the Problems That Are Raised, Even If You Do Not Know the Law:*** We are sure you are tired of hearing us ask you to spot the issues. In fact, often the problem is not the translating onto paper of issues you do spot, but the issues you do not spot. How can you write about an issue that you do not spot? As part of your outlining process, you may want to draw a vertical line through your page and put "facts" on the left side and "law" on the other. Make sure you have covered all the facts on the left and jot down what you know the rule to be on the right. If there are facts that are left where you do not know the law, but you know that you must apply this fact in your analysis, make reference to it so that the examiners do not think you missed the issue entirely. For example, if you do not remember that Joe hitting Sam is a battery, you can simply write, "when Joe hit Sam, he committed a tort." Also, allocate your time appropriately: if you know there are three issues, split your time by three.

6. ***How Much Does My Conclusion Matter?*** We have seen students argue their conclusion of law until a fight breaks out. We simply say this: "We do not care how you conclude, as long as you have a fully analyzed legal argument." Why do you think there are always two sides in a court of law? Each side believes their argument is the winning one, so why should it matter what "side"

---

2. *Id.*

you ultimately reach as long as you argued your side well? As stated before, the bar examiners want to know you can apply the law, so the analysis is far more important than the conclusion. This is also why merely learning how to restate rules will not get you a passing score; learning how to APPLY the rules will.

7. ***Be Clear, Concise, and to the Point:*** Write as clearly and legibly as possible. Do not write for the sake of writing. Do not be needlessly esoteric or verbose. Do not repeat yourself and do not use slang, be unduly casual, or use colloquial expressions.[3] One of our students who got a low score on his essay began with: "Diane is going to argue a bunch of things here." The rest of his essay was not horrible, but we do not think the examiners were very happy with his introduction. While the bar exam does not test grammar or a grasp of the English language, it is testing your ability as a future lawyer, and therefore you should strive to write to the best of your ability. Essentially, this means that a well-articulated essay will probably be received better than one that covers the same issues, but is not articulated as well.

8. ***The Million-Dollar Question: Why Am I Taking the Bar Exam?*** Okay, so we did not make the rules, but we can try and shed some light on them. The Board of Bar Examiners knows you have completed your law studies and you have passed the exams given by your school.[4] You are now being tested on your ability to apply what you have already learned to the facts of problems that might arise in your practice, and that in some instances involve more than one field of law. The value of an answer depends not only upon your conclusion, but also and especially upon the evidence it displays of the elements mentioned above.

HOW TO ANSWER AN ESSAY QUESTION

A well-written essay is one that:

1. answers the call of the question,
2. discusses the *relevant* issues, and
3. is presented in a concise, logical, and organized way.

---

3. See *id.*
4. *Id.*

Format

1. Read the fact pattern carefully   3-4 minutes
2. Generate an outline   6-8 minutes
3. Write your answer   24-27 minutes
                                   ____
                                   36 minutes

1.   Reading the Fact Pattern (3-4 Minutes)

Read the fact pattern two times—once quickly to determine the subject area(s) that are being tested and then a second time to spot the facts that will help you write your answer. Each line may contain several issues, so be careful when you read. Also, remember that multiple areas of law can and will be tested in one given fact pattern.

Example:

Suppose while reading the fact pattern you identify that the question is testing your knowledge of common law Contracts, Agency, and G.L. c. 93A. Also assume that the interrogatory asks: What are the rights of Joe, Jack, and Jill? An acceptable opening sentence would be:

> "Joe, Jack and Jill's rights can be ascertained by applying principles of common law Contracts, Agency, and M.G.L. c. 93A, the Consumer Protection Statute."

A good opening sentence puts your essay in focus immediately and lets the reader know right off the bat that you know what you are talking about.

2.   The Outline (6-8 Minutes)

Why Should I Outline When I Never Did Before?

Organization is key! Outlining enables you to quickly identify, in an orderly fashion, all the principles you wish to discuss. Since questions can contain multiple issues, you must practice treating each issue briefly, but thoroughly. It is also crucial to make sure you talk about defenses and damages in your essay. You will never see an argument set forth in a court of law where a defense is not presented or where damages or liability is not asked for.

Do You *Know* How Much Time I Have on This Exam?

We know: you are pressed for time. We have heard this before. Many of you have looked at us like we are a little insane to expect you to spend 8 of your precious 36 minutes outlining, especially since we just had the audacity to ask you to spend 4 minutes digesting the fact pattern. But we think you will forgive us when we tell you what we are about to say next: outlining really saves time in the long run because when you finish outlining you will know exactly what you want to write. In addition, it will keep you organized and prevent you from skipping issues or putting in unnecessary ones. Feel better now?

All Issues Are Not Created Equal

We know that all issues are not of equal importance on the exam, so we want you to "weigh" your issues. We often see two extremes: (1) students who think that every single issue they spot deserves equal weight so they run out of time and do not get to discuss all of them; and (2) students who think that since some issues are only minor, they do not need to discuss them at all or that the law should be "assumed." Neither of these approaches are the way to go. The best approach is to weigh your issues and determine ahead of time if you will talk about that particular issue "a little" or "a lot" and jot down a time frame next to that issue. You have 24 minutes to write, so figure out how you are going to allocate each of those precious minutes!

3. Writing the Answer (24-27 Minutes)

Okay, this is the part that the examiners DO see. The stuff you did in the last 12 minutes is your behind-the-scenes rehearsal. The first thing you must understand is that even though your reader knows the law, you need to write like the reader knows nothing about the law.

Please be legible. It is hard to grade your answer when the reader does not know what you are writing. Do not be overly verbose or esoteric, but do not be flippant or use slang either.

Example:
"It totally sucks that Jimmy won't get his house. He basically got screwed by his greedy woman." *Please do not do this.*

Example:
"It is quite possible, and perhaps probable, depending on how the outcome of the case will be decided by the family and probate court in Suffolk County, Massachusetts, that the ex-husband, Jimmy in this case, will be denied his ability to enter the premises of 123 Landlocked Lane [hereinafter "property"] and, furthermore, may be required to relinquish his alleged rights to ownership of said aforementioned property in order to conform with the applicable principals of family law in this instance and to avenge the alleged and supposed rights of his soon to be ex-wife, Stacey, who claims that aforementioned "property" is now legally within her control,

which is also subject to the outcome and interpretation by the family and probate court." *Please do not do this either.*

A good way to briefly define your issues is by using the words "when," "because," "may," and "since." These words both elongate your answer while saving you time by not having to give a full definition of each legal concept.

Example:
"When Jason hit Sammy, he battered him since the contact was harmful or offensive."

Each section of your essay should end with your damages section.

Example:
"As a result of his being battered by Jason, Sammy can recover damages consisting of ...".

We would like to stop lecturing you now. Are you ready to try out these techniques yourself? Well, please join us for the rest of the book where we show you what to write, and, more important, what *not* to write.

TORTS *[Evaluated in Question 15 As Well]*

Ace decided to have a July 4th party and invited a few friends to join him. He cooked hamburgers on an outdoor grill fueled by a small propane tank and set a keg of beer on the deck near the swimming pool. Toward dusk, several people who lived in the neighborhood, but who had not been invited to the party, arrived. One of them brought a large quantity of fireworks and proceeded to light them. The fireworks display had lasted for about 20 minutes when a rocket misfired, setting the grill propane tank on fire and seriously injuring Frieda, one of the invited guests. Ace did not know who brought the fireworks. As the fire spread, Ace attempted to clear the cars in the driveway so that an ambulance could get through. Chuck, another invited guest who was, by this point, quite drunk, thought that someone was trying to steal his car and, screaming obscenities, started a fistfight that quickly turned into a brawl. The police arrived shortly thereafter and, while trying to break up the fights that had spread to the street, Officer was pushed over, breaking his leg and dislocating his shoulder. Guests began to flee in every direction and a car hit one of them, Paul, as he crossed the street to his car. It later developed that the streetlights directly in front of the house were not working and Electric Company had not gotten around to replacing them. Ace also learned later that the newer version of his propane grill carried labels warning about the risk of fire and had a protective metal shield that fit over the top of the tank. Ace had purchased the grill at a yard sale but had regularly sent the tank to Manufacturer to be refilled. At no time was he told about the warning labels or the protective shield.

What are the rights of Ace, Frieda, Officer and Paul?

Actual Bar Exam Answer Given To Question 1

Score = 7

The rights of Ace, Frieda, Officer and Paul will be evaluated using Property Law, Tort Law and the Uniform Commercial Code ("UCC"), as adopted by the Commonwealth of Massachusetts. These cases will be filed in Massachusetts Superior Court unless there is a diversity issue in which case it would be filed in Massachusetts Federal District Court. **(1)**

Ace

As the owner or person in possession of the premises, Ace has a duty to invitees to warn them of known dangerous conditions on the property. Ace also has the duty to trespassers to warn of dangerous conditions. **(2)**

In this case, the dangerous condition was the propane tank. While Ace purchased the grill at a yard sale, the warranties usually given by a seller and manufacturer do not apply. Under the UCC, when a seller who regularly engages in the business of selling grills, would give warranties concerning the grill and tank. A person who sells goods at a yard sale is not in the regular course of business and is not expected to give warranties. **(3)**

Additionally, a manufacturer is not required to maintain warranties of second market goods that are sold, unless the goods were defective when they left the manufacturer.

In this case, Ace returned the propane tank regularly to Manufacturer to be refilled and that should reestablish a warranty that the tank is fit for ordinary purposes. Since Ace and Manufacturer are known to each other, Ace could reasonably expect recall notices or updated safety measures to be sent to him.

Ace may have a tort claim against Manufacturer for these reasons.

Ace may also be liable for Chuck's actions when Chuck started the brawl he was drunk and the Officer was hurt trying to break it up.

Ace provided the beer and it was foreseeable that someone may get intoxicated and start a fight.

Ace may have had a duty to prevent the trespasser's setting off fireworks. Where it lasted for twenty minutes, he may have eventually assented to the trespassers.

Ace may have a claim against Electric Company, if the failure to replace the lights in front of Ace's house contributed to the accident and injuries. Utility companies have to replace the lights within a reasonable amount of time.

Frieda may have a claim against Ace, as she was an invited guest. Ace had a duty to warn Frieda of known dangerous conditions. In this case, he did not know of the dangerous condition and therefore should not be found liable.

Frieda

Frieda does have a claim against Manufacturer for strict liability. Manufacturer had a duty to warn of dangerous defects of the propane tank to Ace and Frieda was injured due to Manufacturer's negligence.

Manufacturer can use the defense that the grill was bought on the secondary market and that they are not required to maintain warranties.

However, the defense will fail due to Ace's relationship with manufacturer regarding the regular refilling of the tank. **(4)**

Officer

Officer may have a claim against Ace, if Ace was negligent in serving beer. It was foreseeable that someone invited to his party could get intoxicated by consuming beer.

Ace's only defense would be that if Chuck was intoxicated before his arrival.

Officer may have a claim against Chuck. Chuck started the brawl, but that may not be enough to hold him responsible for the officer's injuries.

Officer may also have a claim against Electric Company. Because the Electric Company did not replace the streetlights, it is foreseeable that the Officer may not have been pushed down and injured if the loss of light was a factor in his injuries.

Paul

Paul has a claim against Electric Company for the same reason as Officer. When a car hit Paul, it may have been for the loss of light. It is foreseeable that a car would hit someone, crossing the street when there is no lighting.

Paul also has a claim against the driver of the car for personal injuries, medical expenses and other expenses.

Comparison Notes

Some students may at this time choose to flip to Answer 15, which received a 2, and compare that answer to the answer presented to the same fact pattern above. Others may wish to come back to Answer 1 when they get to the section addressing the lower-score answers. Or, you may wish to simply go in order. Whatever method works for you, we support!

Note to yourself the major difference between the answer in Question 15 and the answer given here. Take a few moments to jot down your thoughts and key difference here:

Answer 1	Answer 15
(1)	(1)
(2)	(2)

Answer 1

(3) _______________________________

____

____

(4) _______________________________

____

____

Answer 15

(3) _______________________________

____

____

(4) _______________________________

____

____

Our Analysis

(1) This is a good introduction. It briefly states what law will be used and where it should be used. This may seem trivial but it is an excellent way to start your essay, and it lets the reader know exactly where you are going. You do not want your reader to have to guess where you are going with your essay.

(2) This is an example of first laying out the standard or rule that is to be used. This is very important since it shows your knowledge of the law. Always do this before jumping into your analysis.

(3) This is an example of how you can be imperfect, but still obtain a perfect score. This section jumps a bit since it goes from talking about the dangerous condition straight to warranties. This section is a bit disorganized, but the essay still got a perfect score! The examiners know that you are under a time crunch, so perfect organization is not always needed for a perfect score on the exam.

(4) Again, this lays out a legal standard and applies it. Short, effective, and necessary.

General Comments

This essay received a "perfect score" on the Massachusetts Bar Exam. This answer is short and to the point. As stated in the comments above, the essay is also slightly disorganized, but this proves that you can receive a perfect score and not be perfect! Remember that the examiners have to read thousands of essays, and the quicker and more succinctly that you can demonstrate your knowledge of the law, as well as the ability to apply it, the better. As you can see, this author caught all the issues, even if they were not all discussed to the same extent. The author "weighed" the issues and spent the necessary amount of time on each issue without skipping over issues or spending too much time on one particular issue. You will start to see a pattern among 7 essays as you read and analyze the next two questions and answers.

CRIMINAL PROCEDURE

Alpha and Bravo were suspected of being terrorists. Each owned a cell phone. Neither had ever been arrested but both had received large deposits to their respective checking accounts from overseas banks.

Federal agents received an anonymous tip that Alpha and Bravo would be meeting other alleged members of their terrorist group near the Canadian border, although the exact location of the meeting was unknown. The group members would be bringing firearms and ammunition. The federal agents decided to track Alpha and Bravo by monitoring their cell phones' location. The agents had been informed that cell phones transmit signals that reveal the phone's precise physical location when it is turned on, even if it is not being used, and that the location of the cell phone could be obtained by sending a signal to the cell phone causing it to send a signal in return indicating the phone's location.

Alpha drove his car toward the Canadian border, followed by Bravo in a rented car. They occasionally talked with each other by cell phone but otherwise initiated no calls. The federal agents, trailing in unmarked police vehicles, frequently lost visual contact with the cars. Several times, Alpha and Bravo left the paved roads, drove onto land marked with large NO TRESPASSING signs and were not visible even to the police satellite tracking devices. About two miles from the Canadian border, both cars suddenly disappeared and the agents surmised that the cars had entered either a cave or a tunnel. On each occasion when the vehicles disappeared, the agents used the cell phone automatic identifying data, supplied to the agents by Alpha's cell phone service provider, to pinpoint Alpha's and Bravo's location, even when the cars were not visible.

The agents continued to monitor Alpha's cell phone location. About three days later, the cars reappeared on the interstate highway. Both cars were stopped and searched. In Alpha's car, police found $15,000 in a case; subsequent investigation verified Alpha's statement that he had withdrawn $50,000 from his bank account several days before. In Bravo's rented car, a search beneath the trunk revealed a false bottom and several assault rifles and ammunition as well as a small quantity of marijuana. Alpha and Bravo were arrested.

Alpha and Bravo wish to challenge both the searches of their vehicles and their arrest. What are the rights of Alpha and Bravo?

Actual Past Bar Exam Answer To Question 2

Score = 7

This question will be governed by Federal Law, in particular, the Fourth Amendment protection from unreasonable searches and seizures. The agents were federal and the incidents occurred outside of the Commonwealth of Massachusetts therefore the Mass Declaration of Rights would not apply, unless one or both accusees are from MA. **(1)**

Generally, the 4th Amendment of the US Constitution requires a warrant for searches and seizures; otherwise they're deemed unreasonable and unconstitutional searches and seizures. **(2)**

Generally, an accused must have a reasonable expectation of privacy of the places searched and/or items seized. The state or government must be acting and generally a warrant is required to make the search reasonable and constitutional. Additionally, the accused must have standing to challenge the search or seizure. Risk of harm and redressability. **(3)**

Home searches and seizures are afforded particular protection. A warrant must be obtained unless an exception applies. An auto is not afforded the same res. expectation of privacy as a home but requires probable cause to permit a warrantless search. Probable cause may be considered in light of the totality of the circumstances. **(4)**

A properly issued warrant requires probably cause, an impartial magistrate, particularly as to person, items and/or places to be searched, and also state of government action.

The "anonymous" tip most likely was not enough to warrant probably cause, rather just a reasonable suspicion.

Border searches are an exception to the warrant requirement. Though the alleged criminals were supposed to be "near" the border, the federal court will have to decide if this warrant exception applies.

The armed and dangerous accusation contributes to the reasonable suspicion and may even increase the facts to prove the agents had probable cause. Peril was presented as a possible outcome to the police and the public.

Generally, a warrant is required for taping and wire taping a phone and tracking the phone. Here, there was no warrant; this may be unconstitutional. However, the police may claim the border search exception, hot pursuit (less likely), and exigent circumstances (less likely too). **(5)**

To track the car the police most likely violated the warrant requirement, especially if the police used technology not available to the public. However, the Supreme Court has established that a tracking device may be constitutionally used without a warrant to track a vehicle.

As the two cars seemingly dodged the police (leaving the roads, etc.) probable case was being established. This disappearing into caves and off road may have elevated the situation to one of "hot pursuit". Hot pursuit is another exception to the warrant requirement and permits the police to search and seize without a warrant if the situation is currently occurring during the commission of a crime.

The agents monitoring for three days cause the "hot pursuit" to lapse and possibly expire.

Both cars were searched. An Auto Exception applies to the warrant requirement only if the state/government has probable cause. The court may deem, under the totality of the circumstances that probable cause existed.

A's $15,000 may be admitted if probable cause was determined to exist. His statement may be admitted so long as it didn't violate his 5th Miranda rights, as long as he was not in custody and interrogated.

B may have an issue with standing because he was renting his car. But standing will likely lie here. The marijuana and rifles may only be admitted if probable cause is found for this auto search outside his wingspan.

Your Comments: Place *your* critique here for each of the numbered sections

(1) ____

____

____

(2) ____

____

____

(3) ____

____

____

(4) ____

____

____

(5) ____

____

____

Our Analysis

(1) Statement of governing law is very important to let your reader know right away what area or areas of law you will be discussing.

(2) General law—this is always a good place to start. Give the general law, and THEN the specific law. Some students make the mistakes of getting too specific up front or stating the exception to a general rule first. It is always best to start with your black letter law, then go into specifics and/or applicable exception next in a step-by-step, logical manner.

(3) This section is disorganized. It should start with government conduct, and then talk about standing, which, for the purposes of the Fourth Amendment, is synonymous with or explained by reasonable expectation of privacy. Then when you have government conduct and standing, there generally must be a warrant unless an applicable exception exists to the warrant requirement. But the reader did not take off any points, because, most likely, the reader thought that the rest of the essay was quite organized. Remember, the reader knows you are under a time crunch, and that you do not have time to proofread. It appears that the student here was able to keep a logical flow pretty consistently throughout his or her answer, and was not penalized for switching the steps around in this instance.

(4) This starts with the general rule then gives the exception or the more specific aspect of the law. That is always the order you want to go in. It is very rare that the examinee should ever start with the exception or go into the specifics of a rule without stating the general black letter law first. If you compare this with the next essay, which got a 7, the examinee uses the same approach.

(5) The writer could have gone into more detail about the exceptions, but given the time limits, this may have been all he or she could do.

General Comments

This essay is a bit disorganized and does not go into enough detail in some respects. However, it still received a perfect score without being a perfect essay! It should be noted that what makes this essay a 7 is a strong knowledge of the law, stating the law, and applying it. In addition, the way in which the examinee went from the general law to the specifics and exception is the order you want to approach in all of your essays. Weighing the issues appropriately, as you also will see in the next essay, will gain you a high score as well.

Note that you will not get a 7 if you do not apply the law. That's a fact. Do not argue with us on this.

DOMESTIC RELATIONS

Husband and Wife were married in 1975 and lived in Massachusetts. Wife, who was several years younger than Husband, was a high school graduate, while Husband had a college degree. During their marriage they had two children, and Wife was a homemaker who was primarily responsible for the upbringing of the children, while Husband provided the family's support as an employee of Acme Corp., a major manufacturing company.

In 2000, after both children had graduated from college, Wife learned that Husband was having an affair with his secretary at Acme Corp. Wife left Husband, taking with her nothing other than a suitcase of clothing, and moved to another state where, after establishing a legal domicile, she obtained a valid divorce the following year. The judgment of divorce contained no provision for the division of marital property. At the time of the divorce, Husband and Wife owned a residence in Massachusetts. Husband owned stock in Acme Corp., where he had advanced to a high-level executive position. Husband was also named a sole beneficiary under the will of his mother, who was then living.

After the divorce, Wife started a small mail-order business, which by 2002 had grown into a highly successful internet company. In 2003, Husband was laid off as a result of a downturn in business at Acme Corp., and he retired on a pension that was substantially less than he had earned as an employee. That same year, Husband's mother died and he received a large inheritance under her will.

Husband has continued to reside in the residence owned by Husband and Wife. It has nearly doubled in value since the time of the divorce as the result of an inflated real estate market and improvements made by Husband since the time of the divorce. The stock in Acme Corp., which Husband owned at the time of the divorce, as well as additional stock he acquired as a part of his compensation since the time of the divorce until his retirement, has declined in value.

In December of 2004, Wife sold her business for a large profit and returned to Massachusetts to be near her children. She has filed a complaint in the Probate and Family Court for an assignment or division of the marital property of Husband and Wife. Husband has counterclaimed.

What are the rights of the parties?

Actual Past Bar Exam Answer To Question 3

Score = 7

The issues will be analyzed under Massachusetts Domestic Relations Laws. **(1)**

Wife (2)

Although wife obtained a divorce in a different state, Massachusetts would be required to give full faith and credit to the other states divorce. In the absence of a separation agreement, which is required in Massachusetts, Wife may have to file her complaint in the state that granted the divorce. However, if the Massachusetts judge accepts her complaint, it would be treated like she was divorced in a Massachusetts Probate Court. **(3)**

A separation agreement would have to be created containing all marital assets at the time of divorce. These include the marital residence, Husband's Acme stock and his retirement account. Typically, marital assets are equitably distributed and the value is that as of the date of the divorce. In this instance, the marital residence has nearly doubled in value. As a tenant by the entirety (how married persons typically hold real property in Massachusetts), Wife is entitled to one-half of the value of the marital residence. Where the value of the residence has increased so dramatically, the judge may allow Wife a one-half distribution of the proceeds of the marital property less amounts paid by Husband after the divorce for principal. If Wife were to get proceeds for the value of the residence at the date of divorce, Husband would be unjustly benefited by the increase in value. **(4)**

Wife is also entitled to an equitable distribution of Husband's Acme stock and his retirement accounts through a QUADRO (a qualified Domestic Relations order).

Wife would only be entitled to Husband's inheritance if he received it during the marriage. At the time of the marriage Husband only had a mere expectancy, as there was no immanency of mothers death. This will not be included in the marital property.

Wife's company would not be considered marital property, as it was acquired after the divorce.

At the time of the divorce, Wife may have been entitled to alimony. Alimony is calculated based on need and income. If Wife had no income she may be able to get alimony. Where there is no existing separation agreement, Wife cannot file a complaint for modification based on her circumstance. The judge has the discretion to award alimony to either party based on need. Wife is also entitled to equitable division of residential furnishings.

Husband

Husband is entitled to one-half of the marital residence under statute in Massachusetts. He is entitled to credit of payments made toward principal making the division equitable.

Husband is entitled to an equitable division of Wife's marital property, if she had any. In this case, she did not.

Husband would receive his equitable distribution of Acme stock and retirement accounts under a QUADRO (Qualified Domestic Relations Order).

Husband is not entitled to Wife's proceeds from the sale of her company. This may be different if alimony had been ordered initially. Husband would have filed a complaint for modification based on change of circumstances.

Husband is entitled to the entire inheritance from his mother's estate. He received it after the divorce, so it was not marital property. However, if the inheritance had been in a trust and Husband received distributions during the marriage and used those funds for marital expenses, Wife may be entitled to some equitable division of the inheritance as it was not a mere expectancy.

Husband is also entitled to equitable division of residential furnishings.

Your Comments

(1) ____

____

____

(2) ____

____

____

(3) ____

____

____

(4) ____

____

____

Our Analysis

(1) You should be noticing a pattern with the opening statements. You are alerting your reader to exactly what area of law you will be discussing.

(2) It is a good idea, depending on how the question is set up, to divide up your essay by party, property, or claim. Make this determination early on and in your outlining phase. This helps keep the issues clear.

(3) The writer presents a concise statement of the rule as well as application to the facts. Again, the author of this essay states the rule with respect to what a separation agreement would need and how marital property is divided. The author then applies the facts to the law.

(4) It is a better idea to start with the issue. For example, the writer could have put "As for the inheritance, wife would only be entitled …". However, this is another example of an imperfect essay still receiving a 7!

General Comments

Again, despite some imperfections, this essay still received a perfect score. Bar examiners realize that you are under time constraints and cannot edit. Notice the short, clear, concise, and relevant statements made by this examinee. There is no precious time wasted and it is not overly verbose. The examinee gets his or her point across and moves on to the next issue.

General Note on Essays That Received 7s

As you may have noticed, all these essays were very precise in stating the rule and in applying the rule. In addition, they did not miss issues and they weighed the issues that they did spot appropriately. This is what will gain you a 7.

CONSTITUTIONAL LAW

Emerald City, Massachusetts (Emerald) experienced fiscal problems. To save money, Emerald outsourced several municipal services, including public safety—police, fire and ambulance to Mutual Services (Mutual), a private contractor of such services to municipalities throughout the country. Emerald has historically provided these basic municipal services to its citizens.

Emerald's contract with the police, fire and ambulance personnel included a "termination for cause" provision and allowed for random employee drug testing. Emerald's contract with Mutual requires Mutual to retain every police, fire and ambulance employee for a minimum of one year, unless the employee engages in conduct that would allow for termination for cause. The outsourcing contract also allows Mutual to conduct random drug testing of all police, fire and ambulance personnel.

Smith, a patrolman with 20 years of service in Emerald's Police Department, was ordered by Mutual to take a drug test. Several other police officers who, like Smith, operated motor vehicles as part of their duties and responsibilities, were also ordered to take drug tests. Smith refused to take the drug test and Mutual terminated Smith's employment immediately.

What are the rights and defenses, if any, of Smith and Emerald?

Actual Past Bar Exam Answer To Question 4

Score = 6

(1) Emerald, under its U.S Constitutional "Police Power" may contract out its public safety services if it is in the best interest of the public. Under the MA Declaration of Rights a state actor or private entity may not discriminate among others in employment contracts. Specifically, under Chapter 151b employment terminations may be protected. **(2)**

Furthermore, the Due Process Clause of the IVX Amendment protects from the derivation of life, liberty or property (here employment) without a hearing and notice.

Here, a contract was formed. Accordingly, in offer, acceptance (meeting of the minds), and consideration had to be present to have a valid contract between Emerald and Mutual. **(3)**

Mutual will be deemed a "state actor" in this situation because it has been granted the express right for the state of MA/Emerald and is subject to the control of Emerald by contract principals. **(4)**

The "for cause" termination clause may be valid. Though, in MA all employment contracts are "at will", generally, this clause may be valid due to the state action and also subject to the protection of Chap. 151b.

Random drug testing is permitted in employment contracts for public safety positions in MA. This is a public policy rationale to protect the citizens of the Commonwealth from improper action by public servants.

Smith's refusal to take the drug test was probably improper. He, as a public servant, is subject to drug tests, even random. The drug tests don't violate Smith's reasonable expectation of privacy. **(5)**

Contractually, Smith may be deemed a mere incidental third party beneficiary of the Emerald-Mutual contract, thus he most likely will not be permitted to sue in contract.

The random drug tests were even more warranted by Mutual because of public policy considerations. Smith operates an auto as part of his job. If he were to operate under the influence, the public would be at risk and in jeopardy of compromised safety.

Smith's termination may be analyzed under three analyses: contract law, U.S. con law, and MA constitutional law.

Contract Law: As previously stated most employment agreements in MA are at-will, thus terminable by either party at any time. Here Smith may sue for breach of contract but Mutual may defend stating that they are a state actor and may terminate due to the public safety concerns (weak argument).

Both U.S. and Mass. Const. require a notice and hearing for deprivation of job (i.e. due process for life, liberty or property deprivation). Smith received no notice nor hearing so he may have a valid constitutional claim against Mutual if Mutual is deemed a "state actor".

Furthermore, in MA Ch. 151b protects from discrimination based upon many protections in employment agreements. Age discrimination may be applicable. Smith has been with the PD for 20 years and is likely over 40 years old. If so, he may have an age discrimination claim under 151b.

Lastly, Smith may bring a claim under the MA Equal Rights Act on the Declaration of Rights because MA's constitution mirrors the U.S. Const. in letter and in spirit.

Your Comments

(1) ____

____

____

(2) ____

____

____

(3) ____

____

____

(4) ____

____

____

(5) ____

____

____

Our Analysis

(1) There is no statement of governing law here, which would have helped this essay. You always want to include a statement of governing law so your grader knows exactly what area of law you are going to talk about.

(2) This starts to jump around, going from the rule about contracting out public safety to whether you can discriminate in employment contracts. Tackle one issue at a time and complete that one issue before you move on to the next.

(3) This starts out very well, describing Due Process. However, there's no proper analysis—is a job offer, or job contract, really a property interest? If you start with a claim, always finish it.

(4) This is good since it brings up the fact that Emerald is a state actor, but we don't know WHY it is important. First, tell the bar examiners what the standard is, or the rule, and THEN do the application.

(5) There are a lot of conclusions here, but not enough analysis.

General Comments

This essay jumps around a lot, and lacks some organization. While all of the issues were brought up in the limited amount of time given, what prevents it from being a 7 is that there are rules without application, and application without rules. In addition, it lacked a statement of governing law. However, a 6 is an *extremely* good score to get on an essay! This essay most likely received a 6 because it spotted all the issues, both the major ones and the sub-issues, in the allotted time, A little bit more application and better organization would have earned it a 7.

WILLS AND TRUSTS *[Analyzed in Question 14 As Well]*

Ted and Margaret divorced in 1990. Margaret continued to live in the condominium in City which they had purchased during their marriage as tenants by the entirety and which they still owned together. Ted and Margaret also owned together 1,000 shares of stock in Beta Corp., which they had acquired during their marriage as joint tenants.

Ted had two brothers, Edward and Frank, and a sister, Sarah. He had no contact with his and Margaret's only child, Danielle.

Ted executed a will in 1998, witnessed by his lawyer and by Sarah's husband, which provided in part as follows:

I. I give the sum of $100,000 to Andrew (my personal assistant) and Belle (my secretary and Andrew's wife) in gratitude for their loyal service to me.

II. I give my one-half interest in the Beta Corp. stock and my one-half interest in my condominium in City to my sister, Sarah, if she survives me, otherwise to her son, Henry.

III. I give the sum of $1.00 to my daughter, Danielle.

IV. I give the rest, residue and remainder of my estate to my brothers, Edward and Frank.

In 2000, Ted gave Andrew an envelope which contained a life insurance policy naming Andrew as beneficiary and a letter instructing him to hold the insurance proceeds in trust to care for Ted's dog and cat, for as long as they lived. Ted also handed Andrew a duly executed deed to his house in Town, which named Andrew as grantee. Ted then took the deed back and placed it in his safe. He gave Andrew the combination to the safe and told him to record the deed after his death.

Belle died a year later, and Andrew thereafter quit his job as Ted's personal assistant. Ted then drew a line through the names of Andrew and Belle in his will and wrote in the name of Charity, a public charity. This change was not witnessed.

Frank died in 2003, survived by a son, Gerald. In 2005, after an argument with Edward, Ted crossed out Edward's name in his will. This change also was not witnessed.

Ted died in October 2006, and Margaret died a month later, without a will. Andrew has obtained the deed to Ted's house from his safe and recorded it in the Registry of Deeds. He has also stated that he will not care for Ted's dog and cat, but instead intends to keep the proceeds of Ted's life insurance policy for himself.

What are the rights of the parties to the assets of Ted and Margaret?

Actual Past Bar Exam Answer To Question 5

Score = 6

The rights of the parties to the assets of Ted and Margaret will be determined after a careful analysis of wills, Family Law and property law as adopted by Massachusetts.

When Ted and Margaret divorced in 1990 the condominium they owned as tenants by the entirety was changed into ownership as tenants in common as well as the stock they owned as joint tenants was owned as tenants in common. **(1)**

When Ted executed a will in 1998 considering that Ted was competent and of sound mind, was aware of the nature of his bounty, and he had the intent to create a will, the will would satisfy all the formalities required by Massachusetts and be allowed as a valid will. **(2)** Massachusetts requires two uninterested witnesses. The issue of Sarah's husband attesting s a witness would not invalidate the will, however it would void her devisee of the one half interest in the Condominium and that portion of estate would pour over in the residue. Henry would no longer be able to take under the will since Sarah's devise is void. When Ted executed a deed to Andrew the gave it to him, although the deed was not recorded it could be argued there was intent on Ted's part to grant the property to Andrew and delivery of the deed to Andrew. The deed to the house in town as put away with Ted's instructions for Andrew to record once Ted had died. **(3)**

The deed being in a safe and not recorded would not provide notice to any parties that an advancement between Ted and Andrew had transpired. However, after Ted's death when Andrew recorded the deed this would give notice to other heirs and parties about the Advancement between Ted and Andrew had transpired. However, after Ted's death when Andrew recorded the deed this would give notice to the other heirs and parties about the Advancement of the property to Andrew and should not be counted as part of the residue of the estate. When Ted drew a line through Andrew and Bill's names he may have made a partial revocation if his intent was to remove them from his will. **(4)**

When Ted crossed out Edward's name, as long as Ted had intent, he made another partial revocation to his will. When Ted replaced Andrew and Bill's names with the name of Charity he may have a attempted to create a codicil which is a modification to an original will. **(5)** However, Codicils require the same formalities as a will and where the name of Charity was added by not witnessed it could be argued upon contest that the addition of charity is invalid thereby leaving the gift of $100,000 to the residuary. **(6)**

When Frank died leaving his son has heir, Gerald would take Franks' share by right of representation. Gerald could bring a challenge to Charity's [please note that this trails off because the writing was not legible]

Danielle as the surviving issue of Ted and Margaret could challenge the will under a fraud or undue influence theory by Andrew and Belle. Danielle could also bring an action against Andrew for the life insurance policy give by Ted and Andrew with specific instructions to u se its proceeds to care for the dog and cat. Danielle would most likely succeed as she would take under Ted's will as his surviving issue if the will was found to be invalid due to fraud or undue influence.

When Margaret died intestate Danielle as her surviving issue would take what ever assets Margaret had in his estate including the condominium and the shares of Beta Corp stock.

Comparison Notes

Some students may at this time choose to flip to Answer 14, which received a 2, and compare that answer to the answer presented to the same fact pattern above. Others may wish to come back to Answer 5 when they get to the section addressing the lower-score answers. Or, you may wish to simply go in order.

Note to yourself the major difference between the answer in Question 14 and the answer given here. Take a few moments to jot down your thoughts and key difference here:

Answer 5	Answer 14
(1)	(1)
(2)	(2)
(3)	(3)

Answer 5

(4) ______________________________

____

____

(5) ______________________________

____

____

(6) ______________________________

____

____

Answer 14

(4) ______________________________

____

____

(5) ______________________________

____

____

(6) ______________________________

____

____

Our Analysis

(1) This is a very good start, although an alternate method, and a preferable one, would be to start with the validity of the will. This, however, states the rule very well, even if the sentence is not the most grammatically correct.

(2) This is a great example of folding the rule in with the analysis.

(3) This is all great analysis, but it's also a run-on sentence. Clearly, the author still got a great score, but you should always strive to make the reader's job easier.

(4) This starts out really well, but ends without a rule. Make sure you fold in the rule when you address an issue.

(5) This is great! This is exactly why this exam received a 6—it lays out a rule and an application.

(6) While this is mostly correct, it misses some of the requirements of a valid will and ALL of them are needed for a valid codicil.

General Comments

Though this paper is not grammatically perfect, and it could be organized better, it lays out all the necessary rules, and applies a careful and correct analysis. A 6 is a very good score. Compare this essay answer with the answers to follow that received 6s and start to note any similar patterns.

EVIDENCE

Joe was driving his car to work when he was struck by a truck and injured. The truck was owned by Corporation and operated by Frank, an employee of corporation. Joe sued Corporation and Frank (the Defendants) in the Superior Court alleging that the Defendants were negligent.

At trial, the parties sought to introduce the following in evidence:

(1) By Defendants, a written report, prepared and signed by Doctor, a physician who stated that he had not personally examined or treated Joe but had reviewed Joe's hospital and medical records, and that it was his expert opinion that Joe's injuries were not proximately caused by the accident.

(2) By Defendants, a copy of a letter that Joe had written to his employer the week after the accident in which Joe stated that he had too many beers on the day of the accident.

(3) By Joe, a portion of the police report which contained a statement by Mary, a pedestrian who had observed the accident, which in her opinion Joe had not been exceeding the posted speed limit.

(4) By Joe, a statement by Frank to an insurance investigator that he had run a red light just before his truck hit Joe.

(5) By Defendants, Joe's criminal record of convictions for (1) assault and battery six years ago, a misdemeanor for which he was fined $500.00 and (2) forgery eleven years ago, a felony for which he served one year in prison.

(6) By Defendants, a witness, John, who knows Joe from their health club and would testify that Joe has a reputation among members of the health club for untruthfulness.

(7) By Joe, a handwritten diary prepared by Joe's wife, now deceased, which described in detail the pain and discomfort Joe had suffered from the accident and which included conversations between Joe and his wife.

The respective parties have objected to the admissibility of the Evidence. How should the trial judge rule?

Actual Past Bar Exam Answer To Question 6

Score = 5

The issues will be analyzed using Federal Rules of Evidence. **(1)**

(1) The court should rule that the written report by Doctor is inadmissible. **(2)** Expert testimony must be introduced by a witness who is qualified as an expert on the stand subject to cross-examination. The report will not be admissible as hearsay not within any exception. **(3)**

(2) The Court should rule that the letter from Joe to his employer is admissible only if the Defendant's lay a foundation for the introduction of the letter and properly authenticate it with witness testimony.

(3) The court should rule that the police report is inadmissible as hearsay not within any exception. It is not the best evidence. **(4)** The contents of the police report may come in only if the police officer that wrote the report testifies on the stand as to the content of the police report. Even though the police report is a business record it is not the best evidence and will not be admissible without the police officer to testify and be subject to cross-examination. **(5)**

(4) The court should rule that the statement by Frank to an insurance adjustor is inadmissible as hearsay not within any exception. Hearsay is any out of court statement offered to prove the truth of the matter asserted therein against the party making the statement.

The statement may come in if the insurance adjustor is on the stand testifying as to Frank's statement. **(6)** It may be admitted as a declaration against interest. **(7)**

(5) The court should rule that Joe's criminal record be inadmissible. They can only be admitted if Joe opens the door as to his character and credibility, if he testifies or has character witnesses testify. **(8)** His assault and battery charge could be admissible to show his character, but the forgery charge is past the 10-year time limit on admissibility of crimes to discredit or impeach Joe's testimony. The only exceptions are in defamation cases or it can come substantively in to rebut or impeach a witness's testimony, not on a collateral matter.

(6) The court should rule that John's testimony be inadmissible, unless Joe has opened the door to his character by testifying on behalf of himself or others testifying as to his character. **(9)**

(7) The court should rule that a handwritten diary prepared by Joe's wife be inadmissible, it is hearsay not within any exception. The contents of the diary may have been admissible if Joe's wife were alive, testifying on the stand, subject to cross-examination by the opposing party. Additionally, if wife had testified under oath about the contents, then it may be admissible as former testimony under oath. As that is not the case here, the diary is hearsay and not admissible. **(10)**

Your Comments

(1) ____

____

____

(2) ____

____

____

(3) ____

____

____

(4) ____

____

____

(5) ____

____

____

(6) ____

____

____

(7) ____

____

____

(8) ____

____

____

(9) ____

____

____

(10) ____

____

____

Our Analysis

(1) This is supposed to be analyzed under the Massachusetts Rule of Evidence.

(2) Numbering the sections in a question like this is key. In addition, notice how this starts out immediately with an answer.

(3) This doesn't adequately explain the rule—why is the report hearsay? What is hearsay? Why doesn't it fit under an exception?

(4) If the examinee wants to discuss both best evidence and hearsay, he or she needs to have separation. We had to read this a couple times to figure out that the examinee was not confusing the two. The separation could read something like this: *The police report will not be admitted because it is considered hearsay not within any exception. Even if there was an applicable hearsay exception, it fails to meet the requirements of best evidence.*

(5) This is an incorrect standard of hearsay, an incorrect application of the Best Evidence Rule, and an incorrect statement of law concerning the Business Records Exception. Police records in Massachusetts do not fall under business records exceptions. Hearsay is still hearsay even if you are available to testify to it on the stand. And best evidence has nothing to do with the police officer being able to testify as to the contents of the police report.

(6) This is not true. Hearsay is hearsay, whether you are the declarant on the stand or not. What matters is the time the statement was made. If Frank is testifying to what he said when he was a declarant out of court, not under oath, and not subject to cross examination, it is hearsay.

(7) Frank is a defendant (party opponent) so it can be admitted as an admission, not a declaration against interest. Hence, in Massachusetts, it is a hearsay exception.

(8) Start out with the rule, not the exception.

(9) Again, start out with the rule, not the exception. If the examinee had defined the rule in number 7 originally, he or she would not have to repeat it but could simply say "as in number 7 above" or the like.

(10) The student starts out using incorrect law. This student does not understand hearsay, and as we will point out in our general comments, it is surprising that the student got a 5 without understanding it fully. Hearsay does not turn into non-hearsay just because the declarant can testify to what he or she said. The diary was written when the declarant was out of court, not under oath, and not subject to cross examination.

General Comments

The organization and writing of this essay is solid, and the student spotted nearly all of the issues. The main problem is the law. This student has a lot of the law pertaining to hearsay completely wrong, but still got a 5, which is a solid passing score. We included this essay in this book because we wanted to show you that even if you are weak at the law, if you present yourself clearly, concisely, and logically, and spot all the issues (i.e., you know it's hearsay but cannot apply it properly), you can still maximize your points.

TORTS

Jack and Carol played golf one afternoon at Golf Course. While playing, Carol accidentally hit some golf balls onto adjacent private property owned by Oscar. Jack and Carol walked to the edge of Oscar's property attempting to visually locate Carol's golf balls. Spotting one of her golf balls under a shrub, Carol walked onto Oscar's property to retrieve the ball. Oscar, who had been gardening when he saw Carol on his property, rushed over towards Carol, carrying a large shovel and yelling: "Get off my property right now or I'll fix you!" Carol immediately started to run away and tripped over a rusted barrel Oscar had left at the edge of his property. Carol fell and was unable to get up. Jack immediately called 911 on his cell phone.

While waiting for the ambulance to arrive, Jack took some practice swings with his new golf club, designed and manufactured by Acme. Acme had specially designed the golf club so that the mid-point of the club shaft was very flexible. During one of his practice swings, Jack's club struck a rock, breaking the shaft and sending pieces flying into Jack's arm and leg causing deep cuts and permanent injury. The golf club shattered exactly at the mid-point of the shaft.

After Jack bought the golf club and before his accident, Acme became aware that several golf club shafts had broken at the same mid-point where Jack's club had shattered. As a result, Acme changed the design of the golf club by installing a small device in the mid-point of the shaft at minimal cost. There have been no complaints about broken golf club shafts in the redesigned models.

What are the rights of the parties?

Actual Bar Exam Answer To Question 7

Score = 5

The rights of the parties will be determined through an application of Massachusetts Tort Law.

Carol committed a trespass when she entered the property of Oscar to retrieve her golf ball. Trespass is the intent to enter the property of another and entering the property. Oscar would have a claim of trespass against carol. **(1)**

Carol could assert a defense of privilege in that she was entering Oscar's property to retrieve her chattle property the golf ball. **(2)**

Oscar has the right to exclude others from his property but it must be reasonable. Living next to a golf course it is reasonably forseeable that golfers will hit balls into his yard. **(3)**

When Oscar charged at Carol he committed an assault by placing her in fear and apprehension of being attacked. This is evidenced by the fact that Carol ran away. **(4)** Under Massachusetts law, the distinction of the duty of care owed to an invitee and liscensee is the standard of reasonable care. A trespasser is not owed any duty of care of unknown hazards of the property owner.

Oscar, by leaving a rusted barrel close to the edge of his property has left a known hazard and it is forseeable that other golfers, as carol did, be injured by the barrel.

Carol has a cause of action in negligence against Oscar. A claim of negligence will arise if there is a duty to protect others from harm. **(5)**

Negligence is conduct that falls below a standard recognized at law for the protection of others. Oscar had a duty to protect even trespassers from known and obvious dangers, hence the barrel.

Oscar breached this duty by not removing the barrel because it is foreseeable that others could become injured. Oscar's actions in not removing the barrel were both the proximate and legal cause of carol's injuries and she suffered damages by being injured when she tripped. Carol can sue for medical bills, pain and suffering and incidentals. Jack has a claim of intentional infliction of emotional distress against Oscar if Carol is closely related or suffered physical harm due to Oscar's actions. **(6)** As stated in the acts, after Carol was injured, Jack continued to hit golf balls. As a result it appears that any emotional distress was not severe and this claim would fail. **(7)**

Jack has a claim against Acme for negligent manufacturing. Massachusetts has not adopted section 402A of the restatement. **(8)** As such, strict products liability is not recognized in Massachusetts but is applicable through implied and mercantibility warranties under the uniform commercial code.

As a result, Jack's claim should be plead in a negligence claims (as discussed on page 2) for negligent manufacturing and breach of applied warranties. **(9)**

Jack also has a claim under the Massachusetts consumer protection act, Chapter 93A. Allowing defective products into the stream of commerce is a deceptive trade practice in Massachusetts. Jack would have to file a thirty day demand letter before bringing suit to comply with the statutory requirements of Chapter 93A.

In a negligence claim, **(10)** Jack can sue for pain and suffering and medical bills. Acme, by changing the design of the club is a subsequent remedial measure and could not be used in court by Jack as evidence of negligence. It would be required that Jack prove the golf club was defective when it was manufactured by Acme.

Your Comments

(1) ____

____

____

(2) ____

____

____

(3) ____

____

____

(4) ____

____

____

(5) ____

____

____

(6) ____

____

____

(7) ____

____

____

(8) ____

____

____

(9) ____

____

____

(10) ____

____

____

Our Analysis

(1) This is slightly redundant, as it just states the rule and then restates the claim without any application. A better approach would have been to state the rule, then apply the facts.

(2) This is not a defense to trespass. Be sure that if you bring up defenses, they are both correct and relevant to the facts.

(3) This is not relevant, so putting it in is merely a waste of time. It is not a defense, nor does it negate the original claim. Irrelevant information works against you in two ways: first, you do not have time, and second, you want the bar examiners to know that you can pinpoint the relevant issues.

(4) Good rule and application.

(5) The organization here is hard to follow. State the rule for negligence, then the various elements that apply. Here the reverse was done.

(6) Here, the author is thinking of negligent or reckless infliction of emotional distress. Be careful that you are applying the correct rules.

(7) Do not address irrelevant claims, for the same reasons stated above.

(8) Do not give a number of a statute or restatement without explaining what that statute or restatement is. Bar examiners do not have these numbers memorized, and even if they do, you want them to know that you know the rules.

(9) Be sure to always apply facts to law, not just state the law.

(10) Be sure to stay organized. The author began talking about negligence, and then went on to 93A and back to negligence. Finish one claim before starting another.

General Comments

If the organization had been better with a consistent application of the rules to the facts, this would have been a higher score. Remember, a 5 is a solid passing score! The examinee here had a very solid grasp of all of the issues and spotted almost all of them; however, he or she needed to apply them consistently and in an organized manner.

CRIMINAL LAW AND PROCEDURE

Ben usually spent his nights at Hope House, a homeless shelter in City. On his way to Hope House one night, Ben stopped at Convenience Store. Tom, Convenience Store's manager, followed Ben as he walked down the aisles. Ben stuffed a can of soda and a candy bar in his jacket pockets, and as he began to leave the store, Tom grabbed Ben by the jacket collar. Ben whirled and swung at Tom's head. Tom fell backward, hit his head on the floor breaking his neck and died instantly. Jane, who was putting gas in her car at Convenience Store's pumps, watched as Ben began running from the store. Ben ran toward Jane, pushed her to the ground, jumped into Jane's car and drove away. Jane's car contained her designer purse valued at $225, and her infant daughter, Elsie, who was in a car seat in the backseat of the car. When Ben saw Elsie, he stopped the car, grabbed the purse and ran. The purse contained $100 in cash and credit cards.

Jim, an off-duty City police officer, volunteered at Hope House by driving the shelter's van to pick up homeless people in City. Jim carried his gun in accordance with the City police department's regulation, which required officers to carry their firearms at all times. Earlier that night, Jim heard a radio report that Convenience Store's manger had been killed. Ben was sleeping on a park bench when Jim approached him in the van. Jim asked Ben why he was sleeping outside on such a cold night. Ben mumbled something that Jim did not understand. Jim told Ben to get into the van but Ben refused. Jim then exited the van, took Ben by the arms and forced Ben into the van. When Ben was in the van, Jim asked what Ben had done that night. Ben blurted out "I'm a thief, not a killer, I never hurt nobody." Jim locked the van's doors but Ben, in a frantic effort to escape, struck Jim on the head, smashed a van window and opened the van door from the outside and ran away. Jim ran after Ben and grabbed his lower legs, causing Ben to fall. Jim drew his gun, pointed it at Ben and again asked Ben what he had done that night. Ben responded, "So, I'm a thief. I'm not a killer. I never hurt nobody. But he grabbed me first." Jim then read Ben his *Miranda* rights and took him to the police station.

What crimes have been committed by Ben?

What rights and defenses may Ben assert and with what success?

Use this space to try your hand at a sample outline, and then take a look at ours. Remember, if your outline is not the same as ours, that's okay. Ours are just samples.

Sample Outline 1:

Outline Question 8

Crimes:

larceny → can of soda + candy bar in pockets
↳ taking away ✓ of another ✓
— intent ✓

Manslaughter/murder → Tom dying
• no felony   • intent? no
• intent to cause serious bodily harm?
↳ self defense — Tom grabbed shoulder,
Shopkeeper's privilege?
reasonable?

Robbery → Jane's car + purse
larceny ✓ (taking away, intent, another)
force ✓ — pushed Jane (purse +
car
separate?)
✶ also carjacking?
Kidnapping → daughter in car
defense — no intent, didn't see
her

False Imprisonment → Jim forced Ben into van
defense - police/arrest, where is
PC?

battery → struck Jim on head
defense = self defense?

Sample Outline 2:

Outline Question 8

{Crimes + Defenses of Ben}

Facts	Law
1. Ben stops @ store on way to Hope House, Tom follows him down aisle	1. ______
2. Ben steals soda + candy	2. larceny
3. Tom grabs Ben by collar	3. Shopkeeper priv?
4. Ben swings @ Tom's head	4. Manslaughter? murder? Self defense?
5. Tom falls ⇒ dies	5. ⤴
6. Jane sees Ben run away; Ben pushes Jane and takes car.	6. Robbery (larceny + force) carjacking?
7. Car has $225 purse; Baby	7. kidnapprg? NO intent
8. Ben takes purse ($100 cash + cc) and runs; leaves baby Elsie	8. ______
9. Jim (off duty cop; can carry gun; drives van for Hope House) gets report of store killing	9. ⎫ acting as police officer?
10. Sees Ben, asks why sleeping outside; asks Ben to get in van Ben→"NO"	10. ⎬ → false imprisonment? Arrest?
11. Jim forces Ben→van	11. ⎭ Probable cause ????
12. Jim asks Ben in van questions	12. ⎫ Interrogation (custodial)?
13. Ben "blurts" out he's thief, not killer	13. ⎬ not free to leave? confession?
14. Jim locks van doors	14. Did Ben think free to leave by?
15. Ben strikes Jim; smashed van window, runs.	15. Battery → Self defense?
16. Jim pursuit - grab Ben legs — Ben fall	16. "Hot pursuit?" Battery? Reas suspicion?
17. Jim points gun, questions Ben.	17. Interrogation; not free to leave,
18. Ben → repeats, "but he grabbed me first"	18. coerced confession?

Actual Bar Exam Answer To Question 8

Score = 4

The crimes that Ben may have committed and the rights and defenses available to Ben will be determined after a carefully analysis of Criminal law and Criminal procedure as it has been adopted by Massachusetts. **(1)**

Since Ben usually spent his nights at a homeless shelter, it could be reasonably inferred that Ben had very limited funds. Therefore, when he entered convenience store, Tom may have had reasonable suspicion that Ben had no money to pay for anything in the store **(2)**

When Ben stuffed a can of soda and a candy bar in his jacket and began the act of leaving the store without paying, he may have committed a larceny if he had an intent to steal when he entered the store. **(3)**

As Tom followed Ben, when Tom grabbed Ben by the jacket, Ben may have been startled by the unlawful touching that occurred by Tom's act of grabbing the jacket, causing Ben to react in a self defense manner. When Ben swung at Tom, Ben was using force reasonable to fend off what Ben may have thought was an attack on him. **(4)**

Ben may have committed involuntary manslaughter when Tom fell backwards and hit his head on the floor, he died from injury of his neck breaking. As this occurred during Ben's commitment of an unlawful act. Ben may claim that he had no intent to steal when he entered the store and that his actions towards Tom where in self –defense after Tom grabbed his jacket collar and therefore these defenses should relieve him of criminal liability. **(5)**

In the alternative, when Ben entered convenience store, if he had the required mens rea to steal then he would have committed a larceny when he stuffed the can of soda and candy in his jacket. Where larceny is a felony **(6)**, anything that happened afterward could be considered part of the felony. Therefore when Ben swung at Tom causing Tom to fall to the floor and break his neck and die, Tom's death could be a felony murder.

When Ben exited the convenience store and ran towards Jane, pushing her to the ground, these acts may constitute an assault and aggravated battery. However, where Jane's purse containing cash and credit cards were in her car and Jane was standing next o the car when Ben jumped into it, the battery would merge into a robber of Jane and larceny of Jane's car.

When Ben drove off in Jane's car with her infant daughter in the backseat, Ben committed a felony kidnapping where the act was concurrent with the commission of the robbery of Jane.

Ben may assert that he did not know Jane's purse of her infant daughter were in the car and therefore he did not have the requisite or specific intent required for both crimes.

However where robbery is a general intent crime the defense of intent may fail and Ben would most likely be found guilty of Robbery of Jane and kidnapping of Jane's infant daughter. **(7)**

Since Jim was a police officer who was off duty when he heard the radio report that a crime had been committed at convenience store, he had reasonable suspicion that Ben may have committed the crime when he asked him what he was doing outside so late.

Jim may have used excessive force when he forced Ben into the van by taking his arms. Since Ben blurted out what appeared to be a voluntary confession Jim had probably cause to lock the van's doors and make a citizen's arrest since he reasonably believed Ben was the one who killed Tom Since Jim was off duty he could not make a valid arrest as a police officer. When Ben struck Jim on the head he caused an unlawful touching and therefore may have committed a battery against Jim, and when Ben smashed the van windows, destruction of property.

Ben may assert that his constitutional rights against false arrest and confession were violated. However, it is unlikely these will succeed as the confession was voluntary and the arrest was not invalid as Jim had probable cause to believe Ben was the perpetrator of all the crimes.

Ben may also assert that because he is homeless he suffers from mental illness that negate any criminal intent and render him unable to understand the nature of any of the acts he committed as wrong. **(8)**

Your Comments

(1) ____

____

____

(2) ____

____

____

(3) ____

____

____

(4) ____

____

____

(5) ____

____

____

(6) ____

____

____

(7) ____

____

____

(8) ____

____

____

Our Analysis

(1) This is a good start, but can be shortened. Remember, you need to maximize your time.

(2) Why is this important? Be sure to ALWAYS explain why you are including a certain fact. What rule does this support? Be sure to always start with rules, THEN back them up with facts, and do not include facts unless they are necessary as part of the rule analysis. Also, it is not clear how the cashier would know Ben had limited funds, or why that should be a reason to suspect him.

(3) Here the rule for larceny is stated incorrectly. The intent to permanently deprive the true owner of the item must be present at the time the item is "taken," not upon the entering of the store. Also, do not use words such as "probably" or "may," as it sounds as if you are unsure of the law.

(4) Why is this important? Basically, this author is putting the defense before the crime, which leaves the reader to wonder why it is being brought up. As stated before, always raise the claim, THEN the defense.

(5) This is a bit disorganized, so it is difficult to determine where the rule and the analysis are. We know we sound like a broken record, but this is why it is important to outline.

(6) Larceny of a soda and candy is probably not a felony. Also, again be sure to think about organization beforehand, as larceny has already been discussed. Redundancy here can cost the examinee points since he or she is missing out on other issues.

(7) Be sure to lay out the rule and the standards. Here the author discusses intent, but never states what kind of intent is required, or why intent is important.

(8) The author is assuming that being homeless is associated with mental illness, which is incorrect. However, even if there was a correlation, this should have been brought up when discussing defenses to crimes.

General Comments

A 4 is that limbo range where there are all the makings of a solid essay (i.e., most of the issues were spotted) but there are some essentials lacking to make it into the solid high score ranges. If you get 4s across the board, you may be in passing shape, but we would rather have you aim for the scores that the previous examinees achieved.

CONSTITUTIONAL LAW

The Medical School at State University ("School") decided in early 2005 to adopt an admissions policy that provided:

(A) Given that five percent of the State's citizens are Native American, School must ensure that no fewer than five percent of the enrolled first year class shall be Native American.

(B) Given that the State's African American citizens have suffered great historical discrimination, all African American applicants will have their college grade point averages increased by twenty percent prior to the consideration of their applications by School's admissions committee.

(C) With respect to all other applicants coming from racial or national origin minority groups that have been historically underrepresented at School, an applicant's race or national origin may be considered by School's admissions committee as a "plus" in a particular applicant's file.

(D) Given the importance of traditional music to all minority groups, all applicants who are accomplished musicians will have their college grade point averages increased by twenty percent prior to the consideration of their application by School's admissions committee.

The application by John, who was white and not a musician, to attend School was rejected in 2006, even though he had a higher college grade point average than many of the minority applicants who were offered admission by School that year. John filed suit claiming that School's admissions policy was illegal, and a few months later moved for summary judgment.

Town had an ordinance making it a misdemeanor to engage in door-to-door solicitation without first securing a permit from Town. Bill heard about John's lawsuit, and decided to go door-to-door in Town passing out a handbill stating that School had a racist admissions policy. The backside of the handbill had a small advertisement for Bill's pizza parlor. Town police arrested Bill for violating the ordinance. Bill moved to dismiss the charges.

How should the court rule on John's summary judgment motion? How should the court rule on Bill's motion to dismiss?

Actual Bar Exam Answer To Question 9

Score = 4

The following question will be governed by Constitutional law as applied in the Commonwealth of MA. The first issue is whether an Equal Protection analysis may be applied in this case. For such an analysis to apply we must determine whether there was appropriate state action. **(1)** The facts state that the school in question is the "Medical School at State University." Therefore, it is safe to assume we have sufficient state action and may continue our analysis.

John must first prove he has proper standing if he is to assert an equal protecting claim. Standing will require 1) injury in fact (stake in controversy), 2) causation, and 3) redressability. The facts state that John was an excellent student and not a musician who was rejected in 2006. There is little doubt John has suffered injury (he was denied a spot by the admissions committee). It also appears that the school's admission policy was the cause of John's denial. Finally, the courts have the authority and wherewithal to redress this injury. Therefore, since standing has been sufficiently met, and the issue is ripe (harm occurred) John may continue with his lawsuit. **(2)**

(A) Alienage is examined under strict scrutiny by the courts. The standard in the following: Is the statute necessary to achieve an important government interest? And, is it narrowly tailored in its means of doing so. Here, the school has put in place a policy which has a "quota system." That is, no fewer than 5% of the enrolled first year class shall be Native American. Such a quota system is not allowed and will be struck down by the courts. **(3)**

(B) Race is another suspect classification that comes under strict scrutiny in the Equal Protection analysis. If one group us being burdened while another is being benefited such an analysis will be appropriate. Courts generally do not allow vestiges of past discrimination to be remedied as they are being under this policy. Here, the policy is unfairly boosting African American applicants by 20%. Such an action unfairly benefits one group over another and will be struck down by the court. **(4)**

(C) In contract, adding a "plus" factor to minority applicants is an appropriate way to remedy past discrimination. Therefore, this policy will be upheld as valid. **(5)**

(D) Accomplished musicians having their grade point averages increased will also likely be unfair. However, this may also be looked at as a "plus" in an applicant's file.

Therefore, the court should deny school's motion for summary judgment as it is clear that some of their policies do not pass constitutional scrutiny, and unfairly benefit certain groups while placing burden on John. **(6)**

As to Bill's motion to dismiss we must consider whether going from door to door with such pamphlets is protected speech. Bill's communication is content neutral. He is stating that school has a racist admissions policy. Since he is doing such in public then time, place, manner restriction must be appropriate. The test is 1) content neutral, 2) narrowly tailored, 3) with alternate means of communication. Clearly there are other ways that Bill could go about conveying his message therefore the ordinance appears to be narrowly tailored and should be upheld.

As to the advertisement for Bill's pizza parlor that doesn't appear to be unlawful or misleading and is therefore protected commercial speech assuming it satisfies the test.

In conclusion, Bill's motion to dismiss the charges should be denied. Assuming the ordinance was published, and Bill was put on notice that such door to door solicitation was prohibited.

Your Comments

(1) ____

____

____

(2) ____

____

____

(3) ____

____

____

(4) ____

____

____

(5) ____

____

____

(6) ____

____

____

Our Analysis

(1) This is poor organization and poor analysis. For there to be standing there needs to be state action, but the whole point of the analysis should be whether there is appropriate state action. First you state the potential claim, which is equal protection, and then decide whether the state acted appropriately.

(2) This is a great analysis! The author lays out the rule very simply, and applies the facts. This is what should be done ALWAYS.

(3) Here the author has the correct standard of law, and the correct conclusion, but no analysis. The MOST important part of a bar exam essay is the analysis because it lets the bar examiners know that you are proficient in practicing law, not merely memorizing rules and coming up with a lucky guess for a conclusion. Anyone can memorize rules of law, but it takes a lawyer to know what to do with them.

(4) Again, the author came to the right conclusion, but without a clear definition of a legal standard, or a clear analysis.

(5) Here, the author needs to write more. There is no legal standard, nor is there an explanation as to why the result is different here. Also, by "contract" we are sure the author means "contrast." This is an easy mistake to make, especially considering the time constraints, but again, you want to make your writing as clear as possible.

(6) The author needs to put forth a legal standard. He or she has also come to the wrong conclusion, but more important than that, has failed to articulate a rule.

General Comments

This essay needs to set forth the rule, analysis, and conclusion. The author always seems to do one without the others. The author got a 4 because he or she spotted all the relevant issues, but could have gotten much a higher score had he or she followed some of the suggestions in the analysis, especially considering the conclusions were correct. If you are lucky enough to know the law really well, and to be able to come to correct conclusions, you do NOT want to lose points by excluding an analysis.

CONTRACTS

Comppart, Inc., was in the business of selling "aftermarket" computer parts under its own brand name. Comppart bought the parts from several manufacturers and then sold them at retail at its numerous outlet stores. Because Comppart wanted uniformity of packaging, it required the manufacturers to purchase the packaging for the parts from Big-Pak Corp. Comppart gave Big-Pak specifications for the labeling and art work for the packages. From time to time, Comppart itself purchased the packaging from Big-Pak for direct catalogue sales to retail customers. Big-Pak billed Comppart for such packaging, and billed the various manufacturers separately. By 2000, consumer demand for Comppart products had grown substantially. The manufacturers were making greatly increased demands on Big-Pak for the packaging, with the result that Big-Pak's regular, 30-day inventory was not enough to meet demand. Big-Pak's chief salesperson called Comppart's purchasing manager and said that Big-Pak would have to carry a 60-day inventory in order to keep up with demand. The purchasing manager told the salesperson, "Don't worry, Comppart will cover payment for unsold inventory if it becomes obsolete." Big-Pak accordingly stockpiled a 60-day inventory. Shortly thereafter, Comppart hired a new purchasing manager who designed a completely new package for the products, entered into a written contract with Big-Pak's chief competitor for the work, and told the manufacturers that they had to start using the new packaging immediately. At that time, several manufacturers, as well as Comppart itself, had outstanding invoices from Big-Pak for packaging materials already delivered. In addition, Big-Pak had a now obsolete 60-day inventory valued at about $250,000. Big-Pak has demanded that Comppart pay its outstanding invoice and pay for the unusable inventory and that the manufacturers pay the bills submitted to them.

What are the rights of the parties?

Actual Bar Exam Answer To Question 10

Score = 4

The rights of the parties will be determined by analysis of contracts and agency laws. Big-Pak may argue that Compport has breached its duty under a bilateral contract. **(1)** Since Big Pak and Compport are engaged in the business of supplying goods to consumers they are probably merchants and their agreements are probably governed by the UCC as adopted in Mass. **(2)**

Big-Pak may argue that its offer to supply Compport with packing materials and Comports acceptance to pay for the materials supported by the price of the materials as consideration, there was a valid contract. The facts don't indicate a writing so the statute of frauds may be a defense to formation of the contract since the goods are valued over $500. **(3)**

Big-Pak may argue that Compport is responsible for the $250,000 inventory because they relied to their detriment in obtaining the extra inventory based on C's promises to "cover unsold inventory." C may argue that the purchasing manager was not acting within his scope of agency authority when he made the promise and therefore C should not be liable for the $250,000. BP may argue that they were not and should not have been aware that the manager was not acting under comports authority and therefore C should be liable. C may have an indemnity action against manager if he was acting outside his scope. **(4)**

C may argue that it had no contract with BP. BP may argue that requiring the manufacturers to use BP and C itself using BP that an implied K existed through the course of dealing with BP and that BP relied to its detriment on certain promises by C. BP would argue that equity should enjoin C from using BP's competitor and that C pays its invoice and the $250,000. **(5)**

The Manufacturers and Compport may be responsible for the invoices for materials already delivered. BP would argue that each company accepted conforming goods and have not rejected or notified BP of non-conforming goods and therefore the invoices themselves constitute a binding contract to pay for the products. **(6)**

Your Comments

(1) ____

____

____

(2) ____

____

____

(3) ____

____

____

(4) ____

____

____

(5) ____

____

____

Our Analysis

(1) There is no explanation of why this is a bilateral contract. Don't just assert conclusions — as we have told you before, the point of the bar exam is to show your ability to analyze the law. If you are going to assert something, explain why.

(2) There are too many "mays" and "probablys" in this paragraph. You should write with confidence! Stating that the fact pattern is "probably" governed by the UCC implies that you aren't really sure when things are governed by the UCC. We have said this before, but it bears repeating: confidence is key. Even if you are not entirely confident, pretend you are!

(3) Always establish whether a contract exists first, THEN defenses. We realize that the author states that it MAY be ARGUED there is a contract, but you want to come to firm conclusions, THEN bring up possible defenses. However, if you are going to bring up a defense that has "statute" in the name, be sure to define the statute and explain why it applies.

(4) Okay, but what is "agency authority"? If you are going to bring up agency law, tell the reader what it is, then apply it. Again, we have stated this before, but it bears repeating: lay out the rule, then apply it, and then come to a conclusion. Failure to do one of these three things will cost you much-needed points.

(5) This section is repetitive and states principles stated in section (3) above. In addition, there is a lot of "so and so will argue" without explaining why or coming to conclusions. Back up your claims! For instance, why will BP argue that there is no contract, and will they succeed?

(6) This essay ends rather abruptly. Remember to wrap things up, preferably with damages. Do not let the bar examiners think you suddenly ran out of time.

General Comments

There are too many "mays" and "probablys" here and not enough conviction. In addition, the essay received a 4 because it is very difficult to ascertain the rules of law and how they are applied. This essay would have received a lower score, but it caught all of the isues, which is why it received a 4. For this essay to receive a higher score, it really needs more application and conclusions.

A 4 could still be considered a passing score, depending on how you do on your other essays and the MBE, but we'd rather you aim higher than this and maximize your points and hence your chances of passing!

DOMESTIC RELATIONS

Hal and Wendy were divorced in 2004. Pursuant to the judgment entered by the Probate and Family Court trial judge, (a) Hal and Wendy were granted joint legal custody of their minor children, Sam and Denise; (b) Wendy was granted physical custody of both children; (c) Hal was granted reasonable rights of visitation with the children, including scheduled weekdays and alternate weekends; and (d) Hal was ordered to pay child support to Wendy.

In December, 2006, Andrew, with whom Wendy had maintained a relationship for the past year, moved in with Wendy and the children and began to contribute equally to all of Wendy's household expenses. Hal objected to Andrew and Wendy's relationship and to their living together, believing that it would have an adverse effect on the children. Hal's parents also voiced their disapproval, and Wendy thereafter refused to allow the children to have any further contact with Hal's parents.

Recently, Wendy met with Hal and told him that she intended to relocate with Andrew and the children to Ohio, where her parents lived and she had found a better job and where the children would be able to attend very good private schools. Upon hearing of Wendy's plans, Hal became furious and made a threatening gesture to her with his fist, telling her that he would "get her for doing this to him."

Hal has just learned that Denise may not be his biological daughter but rather the daughter of Bill, a man with whom Wendy had had an affair during their marriage. Hal no longer wishes to pay child support for Denise and, in addition, he believes that he is paying too much child support for Sam. He also objects to Wendy's proposed move to Ohio, which will greatly impact his visitation rights and impose a significant financial burden on him, and he would like to have Sam come to live with him, rather than move. Sam, who is now eleven years old, also wants to live with his father and not move to Ohio. Hal's parents object to Wendy's refusal to permit them to see the children. Wendy is concerned about her personal safety in view of the threat made by Hal.

What are the rights of the parties?

Actual Bar Exam Answer To Question 11

Score = 3

The rights of the parties will be determined through an application of Massachusetts domestic relations law.

Hal's Rights: Before Hal's children can be moved out of state, Wendy would have to petition the court for a modification of judgment as entered in 2004. Hal and Wendy do not have a separation agreement, **(1)** therefore his rights to visitation and payment of child support will not be governed by the court order as contained in the judgment. Although Wendy was granted physical custody Hall still has his rights to reasonable visitation moving the children out of state would severely impute those rights. Also, Hal should seek a modification of payment of child support. **(2)**

When Andrew moved in with Wendy and began contributing to the household, the court could modify its judgment for a reduction of payments. In Massachusetts, cohabitation with another party of a divorced parent could result in a modification if the circumstances have materially changed. **(3)** Depending upon the amount of contribution by Andrew, his contribution to the household could warrant a material change and a modification of judgment for Hal. **(4)**

Hal will have to continue to pay child support Denise pending a disposition of paternity. In Massachusetts, the presumption is that children born to married couples are the issue of the male or husband of their mother. Hal should petition the court for a judgment of paternity and submit for the required blood grouping tests. **(5)**

Although Hal's grandparents **(6)** disapprove of the cohabitation and possible move out of state, the court will not consider this as dispositive to a final disposition. Grandparents are not afforded the same rights as parents under Massachusetts law. **(7)** In an attempt to move out of state the court will apply the best interest of the child standard in making its determination. The opportunity to attend better schools and Wendy's ability to have better employment are factors the court will consider in making its determination. **(8)**

In anticipation of the litigation involved for a modification of judgment, the parties should request a guardian ad litem be appointed to represent the minor children. The best interests of the children would be served by such an appointment.

Wendy should seek a restraining order under chapter 209A of the Massachusetts General Laws. If she truly feels threatened, she should move immediately and bring an ex parte motion to have the order put in place. A modification of visitation orders would also be asked for to prevent Hal from being at her place of residence or other restrictions contained in the order.

Andrew's Rights: Andrew should be made aware that if he is adjudged to be the father of Denise he could be ordered to pay child support in lieu of Hal.

Your Comments

(1) ____

____

____

(2) ____

____

____

(3) ____

____

____

(4) ____

____

____

(5) ____

____

____

(6) ____

____

____

(7) ____

____

____

(8) ____

____

____

Our Analysis

(1) A separation agreement would not govern custody and child support rights. Be careful not only to strive for correct law—issue spotting is key as well. The bar examiners only want you to discuss relevant information. Also, even if this were relevant, the author does not explain why. As we have told you before, the analysis is always key. ANYTHING you bring up should be explained.

(2) Why should Hal do this? Always explain the reasoning behind everything. Do not leave the bar examiners to connect the dots, as they might not do so in your favor.

(3) This only affects alimony and does not affect child support. Remember that each parent is responsible for 50 percent of the child's care, no matter who the child lives with. This is an example of getting the law wrong, which may happen to you from time to time. However, you can make the rest of the essay stronger by avoiding the other pitfalls.

(4) Again, this only affects alimony, as stated above, not child support.

(5) The standard here is correct, but the burden of the proof is on the father to prove he is NOT the father, not the other way around.

(6) They are Hal's parents, the children's grandparents. Do not confuse facts, as the bar examiners want to ensure that you are reading carefully. An outline will help you avoid these mistakes.

(7) This is a true standard, but we want more detail as it leaves the bar examiners hanging. Tell them why this is relevant, and expand on it—if grandparents do not have the same rights, what rights DO they have?

(8) What are some of the best interests of the children? The author names a few, but doesn't go into nearly enough detail. This should be analyzed in more detail.

General Comments

Be sure to organize, as yet again, the less organized an essay is the more difficult it is to follow what the writer is saying. In addition, always apply facts to the rules. For the most part, a 3 essay answers the basic idea, but in most cases is not sufficient to be considered a passing score. Had there been more correct law, and a stronger emphasis on analysis, this would have been a higher score, such as a 5.

EVIDENCE

Ed was charged with assault and battery with a dangerous weapon for stabbing his girlfriend, Mary, during an argument about Mary's relationship with her co-worker, Ted. Early on April 22, Ann, who lived down the hall from Ed, heard loud voices coming from Ed's apartment and heard Ed shout: "This will teach you not to fool around!" Ann then heard the sound of doors slamming from Ed's apartment. An ambulance arrived shortly thereafter and Paramedic found Mary lying alone on the floor bleeding profusely from a stab wound in her side. Mary said to Paramedic, "If I don't make it, don't let Ed get away with this. He's not going to hurt me anymore." While being treated at the hospital, Mary told physician that Ed stabbed her repeatedly during an argument. Later, while still hospitalized, Mary signed a police witness report prepared by Officer stating that she had been attacked and stabbed by Ed during a fight in his apartment on April 22.

By the time Ed's case was called for trial in the Superior Court, Mary and Ed had reconciled. The prosecution called Mary to testify. During Mary's testimony, she denied that Ed had stabbed her, and she also denied that she had ever told anyone that Ed had stabbed her.

Following Mary's testimony, the following evidence was offered for admission:

(1) By the prosecution, the testimony of Ann that she had heard Ed shout: "This will teach you not to fool around."

(2) By the prosecution, the testimony of Paramedic that Mary told her, "If I don't make it, don't let Ed get away with this. He's not going to hurt me anymore."

(3) By the prosecution, the Grand Jury testimony of Physician that Mary told him that Ed stabbed her during an argument.

(4) By the prosecution, the police witness report signed by Mary and containing Mary's statement to Officer stating that Ed had attacked and stabbed her during a fight in his apartment.

(5) By the prosecution, Ed's felony conviction for assault and battery upon a former girlfriend in 2004 which is still pending on appeal.

(6) By Ed's counsel, the testimony of Donna, an acquaintance of Mary and a friend of Ed, that Mary had a reputation for not telling the truth and for making stories up to get attention.

(7) By the Prosecution, Mary's hospital records for treatment of bruises received several weeks before she was stabbed, which contained the following statement made by Mary to a nurse: "I'm tired of being pushed around by men. I've had enough of it. I'm a mess, just look at me."

A proper objection was made for each item of evidence. How should the court rule on each objection?

(8) By the Prosecution, the testimony of Sally, a licensed counselor at the Center, a safe-house for abused women, about statements made by Mary during Center visits concerning Mary's fear of Ed and what he might do to her if she attempted to end the relationship. Sally moved to quash her subpoena, claiming that her communication with Mary at the Center was privileged and refusing to testify. Mary's lawyer also moved to quash Sally's subpoena.

How should the court rule on the motions to quash?

Actual Bar Exam Answer To Question 12

Score = 3

How the court should rule on each of the objections to the admissions of evidence will be determined after a careful analysis of the Federal Rules of Evidence.

(1) The prosecution wishes to offer Ann's testimony of what she heard on the night of the incident. This evidence is relevant to prove that Ed was in a state of mind of a person who upset and about to harm Mary. **(1)** Since Ann is repeating a statement that was made out of court and the statement is being offered to prove the matter asserted, it would be hearsay. However, since Ann lived down the hall from Ed and was perceiving what she was hearing as an argument, her testimony may be a present sense impression which is an exception to hearsay. Therefore, the court should allow Ann's testimony under the hearsay exception of present sense impression. **(2)**

(2) The prosecution next wishes to offer Mary's statement to the paramedics as evidence. Mary's statement would be relevant to show that Ed was the perpetrator. This evidence may be admitted as a dying declaration upon imminent death of the person feared they were about to die as Mary was stabbed she reasonably may have believed her death was inevitable. However, since Mary recovered from her injury and is available to testify the evidence should be exclude as hearsay not within an exception. **(3)**

Another view would be if Mary had made the statement in the middle of the emergency while perhaps she was or someone was summoning the ambulance her statement may be admitted as it would be nontestimonial because of the ongoing emergency. **(4)**

(3) The prosecution wishes to offer evidence of Grand Jury testimony by Mary's Physician. This evidence would be non admissible as it was offered during a grand jury proceeding. This evidence is relevant however to show Mary's then state of mine however, it did not come within an exception as privileged for the purpose of medical diagnosis. The prejudicial effect of this evidence outweighs the probative value and the evidence should therefore be excluded. **(5)**

(4) The police report is relevant as a statement of what transpired the night of the incident. However, police reports are generally inadmissible as there is much room for tampering and falsifying also a police report is an abstract of out of court statements thereby the police report should be ruled inadmissible as hearsay. **(6)**

(5) The prosecution wishes to offer specific acts or instances to prove conduct in conformity therein. This evidence is being offered to prove the tendency of Ed to commit the attack on Mary. This character evidence in a criminal case is not admissible as Ed did not open the door to introduce character evidence which would negate his tendency to commit the attack on Mary. Therefore the prosecution can not introduce this evidence unless it is for the purposes of rebuttal. Therefore the court should rule this evidence inadmissible. **(7)**

(6) The evidence Ed's counsel wishes to offer against Mary would be irrelevant as Mary was stabbed and since an injury does not lie and it is highly unlikely that Mary stabbed herself the testimony of Donna attacking Mary's credibility is a inadmissible as Mary's character is not at issue. **(8)**

(7) The hospital records are relevant where they are being offered to show a pattern of abuse by Ed. Since they are being offered to show previous injuries to Mary outside the night of the alleged stabbing they are inadmissible unless they are used to show current medical/physical condition for the purpose of medical diagnosis or treatment. Therefore the medical records should be admitted. However, the statement of the nurse should be severed and not admitted as hearsay without an exception.

(8) Since the Federal Rules of Evidence does not recognize a social worker/counselor and patient privilege the court may follow he rules of the state if Massachusetts has adopted a social worker/patient privilege. **(9)** Since I believe Massachusetts has adopted such a privilege since domestic abuse of woman has become an increasingly disturbing issue the court should quash the motion to subpoena Sally's testimony. **(10)**

In another view, if Mary and Ed are husband and wife Mary by denying Ed harmed her may be asserting her marital privilege as to what happened between husband and wife. However, in domestic abuse cases in Massachusetts the prosecution does not need the testimony of the wife to prosecute the husband for abuse so the criminal case can still continue regardless of Mary's denial of the stabbing. **(11)**

Your Comments

(1) ____

____

____

(2) ____

____

____

(3) ____

____

____

(4) ____

____

____

(5) ____

____

____

(6) ____

____

____

(7) ____

____

____

(8) ____

____

____

(9) ____

____

____

(10) ____

____

____

(11) ____

____

____

Our Analysis

(1) Be careful how you describe relevance—the prosecution is most likely trying to prove that Ed stabbed Mary, not what state of mind he was in.

(2) The author is correct that this falls under a hearsay exception, but that exception is an admission, not a present sense impression. You may be able to argue a present sense impression, though an admission is always a stronger exception.

(3) While unavailability is a requirement for the dying declaration requirement, this misses the issue that another requirement is that it be a homicide charge. In addition, the exception for medical diagnosis should at least be analyzed, yet it was never brought up. In addition, this paragraph is extremely long-winded and difficult to understand. You might have realized, as you were reading it, that you would have to read it more than once. You do not want to do this to the bar examiners.

(4) First address the issue of what hearsay exception would apply, and then discuss whether the statement is testimonial in nature. The author is putting the cart before the horse, so to speak. Even though you do not have a lot of time, it is important to discuss everything that is relevant. However, only the dying declaration aspect was relevant, so it is important to leave out issues that are completely irrelevant. What this section leaves out is the fact that this statement is totem pole hearsay, or hearsay within hearsay. In addition, it neglects to give a clear analysis of the rule, or even a clear statement of any rule.

(5) Here, the rule is stated incorrectly. The common law rule is that police reports are per se admissible as a business record; however, in Massachusetts this is not the case. You still have to take it through the standards of a business record. Here, the author seems to be all over the place.

(6) This would be admissible for impeachment purposes if Ed were testifying.

(7) This would be offered as a prior inconsistent statement to impeach.

(8) Be confident in your writing. Do not let the bar examiners think that you are unsure of the rules of the state you are sitting for the Bar in. Even if you are unsure, be confident, or pretend to be.

(9) This ignores the fact that though some of the information Sally has may be privileged, that does not mean she cannot testify. It is not a privilege against testifying, it is a privilege against communication.

(10) As Mary and Ed are not husband and wife, this section is irrelevant, and you should steer clear of irrelevant information and making up your own facts. In addition, it misstates the rule.

General Comments

This essay could have been stronger with more analysis, in addition to a better knowledge of the rules. Evidence is a topic where it is imperative that you know the rules cold, for both the essay portion AND the MBE. Unlike some other essays we have shown you, and will show you, where the author spots all of the issues and knows the rules, but loses points because he or she fails to apply them, this author lost points for failing to know the rules.

A 3 is generally not a passing score, unless the average for the particular essay overall is quite low. It is hard for us to determine what exactly is "passing" and "failing" since Massachusetts uses a combined scoring process, but in general we want you to aim for a 5 answer to put yourself in solid standing for passing the exam!

DOMESTIC RELATIONS

In 1970, Henry and Wilma, both of whom lived in state X, entered into an antenuptial agreement, with full disclosure by each of their net assets and income. The agreement was negotiated by counsel for each of them. It provided, inter alia, that upon a divorce, Henry would pay alimony of $10,000 per year and transfer to Wilma assets worth $50,000. At that time, Henry had net assets of $100,000 and was earning $20,000 per year. Wilma had neither assets nor income. Under the law of state X in 1970 and through the present, the antenuptial agreement was and is enforceable. The parties were married shortly after executing the agreement and resided in state X for a month. They then moved to state Y where they lived for one year, during which time Henry bought an art works retail store that he gave to Wilma. The store is presently worth $10,000 and generates approximately $1,000 per year in income for Wilma. Wilma periodically visits the store. At the end of their one-year in state Y, the parties moved to Massachusetts where they have resided together with an upper middle class life style. Henry has acquired $1 million worth of net assets and earns approximately $200,000 in income each year. Three months ago, Henry decided to end the marriage. He moved back to state Y where he procured a job, bought a house, registered to vote and intends to remain indefinitely. He filed for divorce in state Y and Wilma was served in Massachusetts by process in conformance with the long arm statute of state Y. She threw the process away. The Court in state Y granted Henry a divorce judgment that incorporated the terms of the antenuptial agreement. Wilma has filed a complaint for divorce in Massachusetts, seeking support and a division of marital assets. By the use of procedurally appropriate pleadings, Henry seeks to defend on the following grounds:

(1) The divorce judgment entered in state Y is binding.

(2) Even if that judgment is not binding, the contract entered into in state X is valid and binding there and therefore must be enforced here.

(3) In any event, under Massachusetts law the antenuptial agreement is an appropriate one and should be enforced here in accordance with its terms.

(4) The appearance of Wilma's counsel should be stricken because he concedes that his written fee agreement with Wilma provides that his fee is $25,000, due in advance, and that he guarantees she will receive an asset division of $500,000.

What rulings should the Court make?

Actual Bar Exam Answer To Question 13

Score = 2

The Courts rulings will be determined by the laws of domestic relations and contracts. The divorce judgment in state Y may be unenforceable against Wilma. Massachusetts will give full faith and credit to other state judgments.**(1)** Henry probably **(2)** obtained a default judgment against Wilma because she did not respond to the action. Massachusetts will probably give the Y judgment full faith because the couple lived in state Y for 1 year, as is the requirement to obtain a divorce in Massachusetts. The court may not recognize the judgment because the couple have resided in Mass for over a year and may require that divorce be obtained here. **(3)**

The antenuptial agreement was probably a binding contract that Henry and Wilma entered into it they were of legal capacity and each intended to make the contract. Henry is probably bound by the agreement to pay Wilma $10,000 annually in alimony and convey $50,000 of assets or else he may be held in breach. **(4)**

Wilma's divorce action may be valid. The Mass court may look at Henry's station in life as well as Wilma's in determining an equitable division of property. The Court may determine which property was marital property and which was individual property for any division of assets. **(5)**

Wilma may only have the art works retail store in Y that Henry gifted to her. Henry probably has $100,000 of individual property owed before the marriage. The remaining property is probably marital property to be divided by the court after distributing the contractual sums.

Henry will probably argue that he is only liable for the contractual sums. Wilma may argue that equity should permit her to receive more due to the large amount of wealth procured by Henry during the marriage.

Wilma's attorney may be subject to discipline for charging an unreasonably high fee and from possibly charging Wilma on a contingent basis that violate the model rules of professional conduct.

The probate court probably has jurisdiction over Wilma's divorce. **(6)**

Your Comments

(1) ____

____

____

(2) ____

____

____

(3) ____

____

____

(4) ____

____

____

(5) ____

____

____

Our Analysis

(1) This is confusing. First, the author states that Massachusetts will not enforce a judgment, then says it probably will. Which is it? And, more important, WHY will it be enforced or not?

(2) Be firm and confident! Words like "probably" only make the bar examiners doubt you, which is not a good way to start out. As we are sure you are noticing, as the lack of confidence in the author's writing style goes down, so does the score.

(3) This is all over the place! The author neither explains the rule nor applies the facts. This is merely a collection of statements. Also, as stated above, there are too many "probablys," which leads a reader to think that the author is not confident in anything and not really sure of the law. This is not the impression you want to leave the examiners with. In addition, as in comment (1), this seems contradictory. Pick one side of the argument and stick with it.

(4) Why is it valid? You always need rule application, and you should lay out the standard for an antenuptial agreement. Here, the author starts to lay out some standards, but does not go far enough. The author talks about the parties' intentions, but there are more requirements that he or she leaves out.

(5) Much like in comment (4), there are no standards. The author is talking about the party's "station in life" but not telling us why. We've talked about "explaining the why" many times, and by that we mean apply the facts to the rule. We cannot stress this enough.

(6) The call of the question is divided in four numbered parts, so the answer should be as well. When the bar examiners give you parts to a question, it is an easy way to organize, so use that to your benefit.

General Comments

This essay received a 2 because it completely lacks any rule explanation or application. Be sure to ALWAYS explain the "why:" put forth the rule, and then explain how that rule applies to this fact pattern. In addition, the examiners gave the writer a specific structure to follow and the writer did not follow it. Consider it a blessing when the examiners give you a structure they want you to follow; do not ignore this. In addition, whatever stance you decide to take, be CONFIDENT. Do not let on that you are unsure of the law, and erase words like "probably" from your vocabulary.

WILLS AND TRUSTS *[Question 5 Revisited]*

Ted and Margaret divorced in 1990. Margaret continued to live in the condominium in City which they had purchased during their marriage as tenants by the entirety and which they still owned together. Ted and Margaret also owned together 1,000 shares of stock in Beta Corp., which they had acquired during their marriage as joint tenants.

Ted had two brothers, Edward and Frank, and a sister, Sarah. He had no contact with his and Margaret's only child, Danielle.

Ted executed a will in 1998, witnessed by his lawyer and by Sarah's husband, which provided in part as follows:

I. I give the sum of $100,000 to Andrew (my personal assistant) and Belle (my secretary and Andrew's wife) in gratitude for their loyal service to me.

II. I give my one-half interest in the Beta Corp. stock and my one-half interest in my condominium in City to my sister, Sarah, if she survives me, otherwise to her son, Henry.

III. I give the sum of $1.00 to my daughter, Danielle.

IV. I give the rest, residue and remainder of my estate to my brothers, Edward and Frank.

In 2000, Ted gave Andrew an envelope that contained a life insurance policy naming Andrew as beneficiary and a letter instructing him to hold the insurance proceeds in trust to care for Ted's dog and cat, for as long as they lived. Ted also handed Andrew a duly executed deed to his house in Town, which named Andrew as grantee. Ted then took the deed back and placed it in his safe. He gave Andrew the combination to the safe and told him to record the deed after his death.

Belle died a year later, and Andrew thereafter quit his job as Ted's personal assistant. Ted then drew a line through the names of Andrew and Belle in his will and wrote in the name of Charity, a public charity. This change was not witnessed.

Frank died in 2003, survived by a son, Gerald. In 2005, after an argument with Edward, Ted crossed out Edward's name in his will. This change also was not witnessed.

Ted died in October 2006, and Margaret died a month later, without a will. Andrew has obtained the deed to Ted's house from his safe and recorded it in the Registry of Deeds. He has also stated that he will not care for Ted's dog and cat, but instead intends to keep the proceeds of Ted's life insurance policy for himself.

What are the rights of the parties to the assets of Ted and Margaret?

Actual Bar Exam Answer To Question 14

Score = 2

In order to determine the rights of the parties to Ted and Margaret's assets, a careful analysis of the facts and will provisions according to Massachusetts Wills and property trust law is required.

The will as executed may be subject to a challenge for lack of proper execution **(1)** since it was witnessed by arguably interested parties, particularly Sarah's husband who is likely to bear some benefit for the disbursement of Ted's estate as Sarah's/devisee's husband. **(2)**

If the will was duly executed, it is likely that Andrew would receive the $100k as directed in the original will since the crossing out of his and Bill's name by Ted before his death were probably not enough to revoke the provision. **(3)** Ted could have crossed out or added a codicil to modify the will, but that would have required a valid execution, with witnesses and all, but this did not happen. **(4)** Since the money was supposed to go to the charity they might be able to ask a probate court to review the change, but that is not likely to change anything. **(5)** As for Ted's divesture of half his interest in Peta Corp stock that is likely to fall to Danielle since upon his death it went to Margaret under joint tenancy right of survivorship, **(6)** and is likely to go to Danielle as the sole living heir to Margaret since she died intestate. The condominium is likely to be split between Sarah and Danielle since it was held in a tenancy by its entirety. Danielle might argue that Ted's half went to her at his death, but that is not likely. Danielle would also get the $1.00 bequest and that might influence the probate court's decision when they devise Margaret's intestate estate.

Gerald is not likely to get the residue of Ted's estate since his father died before Ted and the divestment would have lapsed. Yet as a anti-lapse statute state, Gerald might be able to recover his father's share particularly since Ted's intent would be examined. **(7)**

Edward might still be able to recover something from the estate, but is likely to find hurdles I the court gives any credence to Ted's cross outs.

As for the insurance policy, Andrew is not likely to remain in possession if the proceedings since he obfuscated his duty to care for

Ted's dog and cat. A trust's administration where Andrew arguably is required to only use the trust to benefit the beneficiaries. He can take nominal fees for the time spent and expenses, but not the whole lot of proceeds.

Andrew would not be out of luck totally **(8)** though since he is likely to take possession of the house in Town. Even though it was not recorded until after Ted's death, courts have recognized deeds as duly executed once delivered which Ted did before he died. Any recording challenge is likely to fall bare since Ted asked how to hold off on recording until after his death. Danielle, Gerald, or Edward might lay claim to the Town home, but it is not likely to be lost by Andrew.

Your Comments

(1) ____

____

____

(2) ____

____

____

(3) ____

____

____

(4) ____

____

____

(5) ____

____

____

(6) ____

____

____

(7) ____

____

____

(8) ____

____

____

Our Analysis

(1) Why wasn't it properly executed? What does a valid will need? You always need to lay the foundation of the rule, or the standard, prior to analyzing. This is something that is perfectly acceptable to bring up, but be sure to take issues in a logical order.

(2) Here, the statute is applied incorrectly. The statute requires that if an interested party signs as a necessary witness, they lose their benefit, but the will is still valid. This is called the disinterested witness statute, and it should first be explained, and then applied. The author here did neither.

(3) It is a valid revocation here, but not a valid codicil. So, the gift would not go to the crossed-out parties, but it would not go to the charity either. Also, avoid the word "probably." You want to convince the bar examiners that you are confident in your answer.

(4) First, this should have gone in the essay prior to the sentence before it. As we have stated very many times, lay out the rule first. In addition, language such as "witnesses and all" is far too casual for the bar exam.

(5) What does a probate court reviewing the document have to do with the money going to charity? And why is that likely to not change anything? Again, there are no rules OR analysis here. You also want to be careful that everything you put in is indeed relevant, since you have limited time and space.

(6) This is an incorrect application of the facts. Divorce is one of the things that destroys survivorship rights; ergo, they each own one-half.

(7) Lay out what the anti-lapse statute is and apply it. We have stated this before, but first you have to lay out the rule, and then apply the facts to that rule.

(8) As with "witnesses and all," "out of luck" is too casual for a bar exam essay.

General Comments

Always lay out the rule very clearly, and then apply it. Obviously, to get a good score, it is important to know the correct rules and to apply them correctly. First, however, you must take the time to state the rule. This essay also discusses things that are not all that important to the call of the question, while failing to apply and explain relevant statutes. A 2 is not a passing score.

Please compare this answer to the answer given in Question 5, which received a 6. Both of the students are answering the same fact pattern, but note the differences in each writer's essay that distinguishes a 2 answer from a 6 answer.

TORTS *[Question 1 Revisited]*

Ace decided to have a July 4th party and invited a few friends to join him. He cooked hamburgers on an outdoor grill fueled by a small propane tank and set a keg of beer on the deck near the swimming pool. Toward dusk, several people who lived in the neighborhood but who had not been invited to the party arrived. One of them brought a large quantity of fireworks and proceeded to light them. The fireworks display had lasted for about 20 minutes when a rocket misfired, setting the grill propane tank on fire and seriously injuring Frieda, one of the invited guests. Ace did not know who brought the fireworks. As the fire spread, Ace attempted to clear the cars in the driveway so that an ambulance could get through. Chuck, another invited guest who was, by this point, quite drunk, thought that someone was trying to steal his car and, screaming obscenities, started a fistfight that quickly turned into a brawl. The police arrived shortly thereafter and, while trying to break up the fights that had spread to the street, Officer was pushed over, breaking his leg and dislocating his shoulder. Guests began to flee in every direction and a car hit one of them, Paul, as he crossed the street to his car. It later developed that the streetlights directly in front of the house were not working and Electric Company had not gotten around to replacing them. Ace also learned later that the newer version of his propane grill carried labels warning about the risk of fire and had a protective metal shield that fit over the top of the tank. Ace had purchased the grill at a yard sale but had regularly sent the tank to Manufacturer to be refilled. At no time was he told about the warning labels or the protective shield.

What are the rights of Ace, Frieda, Officer and Paul?

Actual Bar Exam Answer To Question 15

Score = 2

Ace

May be liable to Frieda in negligence. **(1)** Ace owes a duty of reasonable care to his invitees. **(2)** Ace can argue he did not breach that duty because the tank exploded due to the fireworks and that the uninvited guest who caused the injury to Frieda was a trespasser and therefore he is not responsible for trespassers acts. **(3)** He may also argue that the Manufacturer should be held liable because the tank was defective and under UCC warranties in Mass the manf. would be held "strictly" liable for the explosion. Although manf. may argue that buying the grill at the yard sale cut off manf.'s liability because manf. did not place the defective product into the stream of commerce. Manf. would also argue that warning label was sufficient and did not make the grill defective. Manf. may argue Ace assumed the risk of using the grill without warnings.

Freida

May try and recover for injury from Ace, as the owner of the land and host and that he is responsible for al injuries. Freida may also assert a claim of negligence against Manufacturer. **(4)**

Officer

He may have a claim against Chuck for battery for his injuries. He may claim that Chuck's offensive touching was transferred to him and also that the police was a reasonably foreseeable person. **(5)** If officer asserts a claim against Ace, Ace may again defend that he is not liable for the intentional torts of trespassers on his land. **(6)** Officer may argue that Ace should have been aware that trespassers would come to the party in his neighborhood and should have reduced the risk for any negligent acts or intentional torts.

Paul

May assert a negligence claim against Electric Company for his injuries if he can should they owed a duty to Paul and that he was not 51% comparative negligent in running into the street. Paul may have a claim against Ace since Paul was an invited guest [illegible] in negligence and also against Manufacturer.

Electric Company may assert the driver of the car was 51% negligent to absolve Electric from liability or that Paul or driver was comparatively negligent for a reduction in damages.

Chuck may also be guilty of criminal battery for the offensive contact of the fistfights.

Manufacturer may also assert that the burden to place warnings and shields on all older model grills out weigh the risk and therefore should not be held liable on injuries caused by the explosion. Also, all those injured assumed the risk of staying for 20 minutes to watch the fire works that a reasonable person would have appreciated the risk and left the area.

Your Comments

(1) ____

____

____

(2) ____

____

____

(3) ____

____

____

(4) ____

____

____

(5) ____

____

____

(6) ____

____

____

Our Analysis

(1) Be sure to use complete sentences. The bar examiners are not looking for grammar mavens, but they need to understand what you are saying. In addition, do not use words like "probably." A better way to state this would be to say "Frieda will be liable to Ace for negligence."

(2) Okay, we have the duty of care, but WHY is that important? Tie this back to negligence somehow, as in "the first element required is …".

(3) Where is the rule here? Remember, always state a rule, even if you think it is obvious. You also want to explain why this ties into duty. Again, even if it seems obvious, tie everything together. Look at it like showing your work in math problems—it's boring, but it has to be done.

(4) Why? Where are the standards? What happened? Where are the applications of the rule to the facts? This really does not state anything, so it is not helpful to the bar examiners.

(5) We don't yet have a standard. ALWAYS put the rule, statute, or standard first. We have said this many times, but it bears repeating.

(6) Here, the author has raised a defense without telling the bar examiners what the claim was, or if the claim was met. In every instance, you want to first fully analyze a potential claim that the plaintiff has, and then, and only then, raise a defense.

General Comments

Remember that this question appears at the beginning of this book as Question 1, but the student who wrote that answer received a perfect 7 score. *You should compare and contrast the 7 answer given in Answer 1 with the 2 answer given here.*

PROPERTY

Tim's father owned Black Acre in fee simple absolute, a one acre parcel of land with a house and garage situated thereon. In 1974, Tim acquired his interest in Black Acre via a duly executed and recorded deed from his father. The father's deed conveyed Black Acre to Tim subject to the following condition: "to my son Tim for so long as he remains married and if he should divorce, the ownership is to be shared by Tim and my daughter, Mary." Tim's father died testate in 1986 and left all of his property to Tim. Mary is still alive. Tim, the present record owner, is married but presently separated and has entered into a written purchase and sale agreement with Jack and Diane. Jack and Diane are unmarried friends who are interested in purchasing the property and living together. According to the terms of the contract, Tim is to convey "a marketable and good and clear record title subject to restrictions and encumbrances of record which do not interfere with the use of Black Acre for residential purposes." The contract was signed by the parties on February 1, 2004, and the delivery of the deed was scheduled for May 1, 2004. The agreed upon selling price was $680,000. Jack and Diane were to take title as joint tenants. Tim held the deposit of $68,000. A neighbor of Black Acre informed Jack and Diane that years ago toxic waste was dumped on Black Acre and that the property occasionally emits a strong odor. According to the neighbor, Tim was aware of this but the odor continued, especially in warm weather, thereby limiting use of the property. On April 15, 2004, Jack died, devising his real estate to his friend, Ed, and bequeathing his personal property to another friend, Betty. On April 25, 2004, Diane notified Tim that she would not proceed with the purchase of Black Acre and demanded a refund of the $68,000 deposit. Tim refused Diane's demand for the return of the deposit and intends to proceed with the sale.

What are the rights of the parties?

Actual Bar Exam Answer To Question 16

Score = 2

Diane is going to argue a bunch of things here.**(1)** First she is going to argue that the property is not marketable title, because Tim's sister Mary has a future interest in the property which may even come into being soon because is separated and may even get divorced which would partial David his interest in Black acre due to Mary's executory interest. If ones estate has too many future interest in it, it can be argued that the title can not be marketable. **(2)**

On the other hand, Tim may wish to argue that he can provide marketable title. He could get his sister Mary's interest conveyed to him. It is only one person, which would be a lot easier than if there were many other future interests to Black acre. It must be noted that marketable title is implied, and need not be stated in the contract or deed. **(3)**

Something that Tim is going to argue is that Diane now owns Black acre through the doctrine of conversion, even though it would be a weak argument, because the doctrine usually applies when the property is destroyed, but Tim may argue that the property is now unmarketable because of the stench (he'll have to convince that he didn't know). Therefore, because the contract was signed, Diane now owns the property in equity. **(4)**

On the other hand, Diane may wish to pursue a contract action because Tim misrepresented the defeat of the odor, which he had a duty to reveal because it is material and probably would have changed Jack and Diane's mind about buying the property. It should have been made aware to them. Tim broke the duty of fair dealing that is implied in Contracts, along with misrepresentation. **(5)**

Because Jack and Diane were supposed to get title to the property as joint tenants, one could argue that Diane would own the whole property of Black acre because she had a right of survivorship and Ed would not get any though he inherited Jack's realty. Ed should argue that the element of time in a joint tenancy between Jack and Diane will not be concurrent, therefore he should get a piece of Black acre as a tenant in common with Diane.

Your Comments

(1) ____

____

____

(2) ____

____

____

(3) ____

____

____

(4) ____

____

____

(5) ____

____

____

Our Analysis

(1) First and foremost, do not *ever* start your answer like this. We know this student and he is very bright, but in addition to being far too casual, this statement does not actually say anything. Diane is going to argue a bunch of things? Really? We should hope so. Just start your essay, and try not to anger the reader with an introductory sentence like this. Yet again, this is where "writing like a lawyer" comes in. While the examiners are grading you on the law, how you present the law can influence their overall judgment.

(2) This actually does not make much sense. While the bar examiners do not take away points for grammar and sentence structure per se, they do need to be able to understand what you are conveying. We have said it before, but the more articulate you are, and the easier your essay is to read, the higher your score will be.

(3) Where are the rules? It seems as if the author is just discussing facts, with no rules of law. We have said many times that the important part is the ANALYSIS, but the bar exam IS a legal exam. Please put in some law, THEN analyze. While it is true the analysis is the most important part, you first need to state a rule.

(4) What is the rule for conversion? How will that apply? ALWAYS give a rule, explain the rule, and then apply facts.

(5) Yet again, what is the rule? Where are the standards? Do not leave your reader guessing! Connect the dots for the reader.

General Comments

This essay is far too casual and doesn't actually give any rules of law, which is necessary, since you are being tested on your knowledge of the law.

Overall, this is a heavily issue-laden question because it tests your knowledge on future interests (as well as Massachusetts specific law on fee simple determinable and executory interests); marketable title; land sale contracts (including when a party can rescind); joint tenancies; and obligations, rights, and liabilities prior to and post closing. This is the kind of essay where outlining is crucial in order to maximize your points because each issue builds on the way you analyze the previous issue.

In case you were wondering, after we instructed this student on what *not* to write on his exam, he passed on his very next try! Remember, all of the students that contributed essays to this book are very bright, and in fact, are now very bright lawyers. We are certain that you have made similar mistakes to those in these essays, so remember to learn from these mistakes and pass!

TORTS

Ben, a resident in emergency medicine at Hospital ("Hospital"), a large private downtown medical center, had difficulty "making ends meet" on his resident's salary and, therefore, moonlighted 2 days a week at Clinic ("Clinic"), a suburban urgent-care "walk-in" facility owned and operated by Dr. White as a professional corporation. The remainder of the week Ben spent serving his residency in the emergency room at Hospital where his hours were long and unpredictable. Ben was paid a salary by Hospital, participated in its residents' program and performed all the duties and responsibilities of a resident. Besides Ben's salary and benefits, Hospital supplied Ben with hospital clothing, instruments and equipment. Ben's performance as a resident was evaluated by officials at Hospital. Clinic paid Ben for "moonlighting" at an hourly rate, listed his name on its directory as an emergency room doctor and also provided him with hospital clothing, instruments and equipment, but Clinic did not provide any other benefits to Ben. At Clinic, as a matter of policy, Dr. White instructed all doctors at his clinic never to promise a patient a result or cure for his or her condition for which they have been seen by that doctor at Clinic. There was no formal evaluation policy at Clinic, but there was a manual for people who worked there. During one of his days at Clinic, Ben examined a young woman named Mary who complained that she had experienced severe abdominal cramps for several days and that the pain was getting worse. Ben diagnosed Mary's condition as a viral gastric disorder, prescribed a mild medication, and assured Mary that she would recover completely and quickly in a few days. The next day Mary telephoned Clinic to speak to Ben because the pain and discomfort had worsened. Unable to reach Ben at Clinic, Mary was directed to try to reach Ben at Hospital. Subsequently, Mary telephoned and visited Ben at Hospital where, after another examination, Ben repeated his diagnosis and assurances of the previous day. That evening Mary experienced unbearable gastric pain and then visited the emergency room at another hospital where she was operated on for a ruptured appendix. Mary sued Ben, Hospital and Clinic.

What are the rights and liabilities of the parties?

Use this space to try your hand at a sample outline, and then take a look at ours. Remember, if your outline is not the same as ours, that's okay. Ours are just samples.

Sample Outline 1:

Outline Question 17

Mary v Ben

negligence < duty - reasonable doc
breach - what reasonable doc would do? more tests?
Causation - but for breach, no ruptured appendix
injury - Surg / ruptured appendix

Mary v Clinic

Vicarious liability - if Ben is employee, Clinic is liable.

employee v. Ind K

- hourly rate - Ind K
- no benefits - Ind K
- directory - employee
- provide tools + clothes - employee
- Dr white supervision - employee

Clinic's own neg? (if time)

Mary v Hospital

Vicarious liability - same above, Ben clearly employee, but was he in scope of employment?

↳ treating patients routine for residents.

↳ She came in specifically for Ben
↳ 1st saw him at clinic

Sample Outline 2:

Outline Question 17

Mary v. Ben, Hospital, Clinic

Facts	Law
1. Ben resident @ Hospital; salary, benefits, etc.	1. Employee; Vicarious liability → Respondeat Superior (most likely)
2. Ben 2 days/week @ Clinic; hourly, no benefits, but Manual and instructions by owner not to promise results. Tools: clothes.	2. Employee or Indep Contractor? (Analyze using facts)
3. Ben examined Mary @ Clinic; promised recovery	3. Outside Scope of employment if employee of Clinic? If not employee, what would reas doctor do?
4. Mary pain gets worse; Clinic tells Mary to call Hospital.	4. Hospital can go after Clinic for Contribution/indemnification? Shows that Ben = Indep Contractor?
5. Mary goes to hospital where sees Ben; Ben assures all ok.	5. Hospital (employer) liability of Ben (employee). Outside scope (Ben)? Clinic responsibility (1st seen @clinic)?
6. Mary goes to other Hospital, Ruptured appendix Surgery	6. Oh oh. Ben did not diagnose correctly. Reas doctor? Negligence.

Actual Bar Exam Answer To Question 17

Score = 2

The rights and liabilities of the parties will be determined by tort law and agency principles of the Commonwealth of Massachusetts.

Mary vs. Clinic (1)

When a patient seeks assistance at a medical facility, it is expected that he or she will be treated by licensed professionals. As a resident, Ben was not an emergency room doctor, as he was listed on clinic's directory. (2) However, by listing Ben as such and providing the necessary clothing, instruments, and equipment, the Clinic held Ben out to be something he was not. There was a duty, as a Clinic, owed to its patients. This duty was breached as a result of one of it's agent's actions, and its own. This breach was the actual cause, because but for the negligent operation of the Clinic in entrusting patient care to a resident, the injury would not have occurred. The actions of the Clinic was also the proximate, or legal cause, as it was foreseeable that this type of injury would result following these actions. And lastly, the ruptured appendix shows the damages, for a cause against the Clinic for negligence. (3)

Mary vs. Ben

Because Ben is also liable for his actions, Mary may succeed in a suit against him. Ben diagnosed, prescribed, and assured Mary of her recovery. (4) This may have been due to Ben's informal training as he held himself out as an emergency room doctor and not a resident. These actions would certainly be considered as within the scope of employment, thus, in addition to the negligence claims against the Clinic and Ben, under the theory of Respondent Supervisor, the Clinic would be also liable. (5)

Ben may have been considered an independent contractor, due to his limited employment and lack of benefits. However, this argument would fail short because of the fact that Ben was in fact listed as an emergency room doctor. (6)

Although Dr. White instructed all doctors never to promise results, Ben did so anyway. Due to the lack of formal evaluation policy, it shows that the Clinic's procedures were flawed in such a way to foster this negligent activity.

Mary vs. Hospital

Mary's claim, if any, against hospital would likely be raised under negligence and respondent superior, as her claims were against clinic. However, other than providing a contact number, Ben never represented that he was affiliated in any way, for the purposes of Mary's treatment, with Hospital. Mary will argue, though, that once she telephoned and visited Ben, and he diagnosed her, at Hospital, he held himself out as a doctor there. Thus, Mary's claim, for the same reasons as against Clinic may succeed against Hospital. **(7)**

Mary may also seek a claim under Massachusetts General Laws, section 93A. This section protects public and private individuals, and provides relief, for unfair or deceptive trade practices in business and commerce. Section 9, of MGL 93A, governs suits against businesses by consumers. It provides that prior to filing a suit, a written demand letter must be sent out to, here Hospital and Clinic, the business. If the consumer succeeds, he or she may be entitled to attorney's fees and costs as well as multiple damages. If the conduct was willful or knowing, multiple, up to triple, damages may be awarded. The conduct must occur in Massachusetts, and the statute of limitations is four years. It should be noted that if the consumer rejects the demand letter, multiple damages may not be had. **(8)**

Your Comments

(1) ____

____

____

(2) ____

____

____

(3) ____

____

____

(4) ____

____

____

(5) ____

____

____

(6) ____

____

____

(7) ____

____

____

(8) ____

____

____

Our Analysis

(1) First, we suggest starting with Mary v. Ben, since the most issues can be raised between those two parties. After that, you can talk about agency and respondeat superior issues, if applicable. This way, the organization will not only be easier for you, but for the reader as well. Remember, even though there is not ONE right way to organize, keeping the organization logical makes it easier for everyone.

(2) The author presupposes that Ben, as a resident, is not a licensed doctor. However, residents are in fact doctors. This is just a case of misunderstanding the facts, and while the bar exam does not require you to bring in outside knowledge, sometimes it is necessary. There will be times when you misunderstand a fact, or two, or ten, but you can mitigate the effects of these types of mistakes by having a good analysis. The bar examiners do not care about your knowledge of medical licensing, but they DO care how you apply facts to the law. Here, the author discusses Ben not being a licensed doctor but does not explain why that might be important, or apply it to any rule of law.

(3) While the author talks about duty, breach, and causation, his or her answer doesn't actually explain what the duty was, or where the breach occurred. Moreover, the answer addresses the fact that the clinic is responsible for Ben's actions, but doesn't tell us WHY. This should have been an employee versus independent contractor analysis. You can probably guess what we are going to say by now: lay out the rule and then apply the facts!

(4) Before you discuss liability, you need to address the duty that Ben owed, whether that duty was breached, and what the causation was. This answer seems to presuppose a breach of a duty, without fully explaining what that breach was.

(5) The clinic has already been discussed, so why go back to it? As we have explained a few times before, this is where an outline comes in handy, since an outline allows you to think about where you want to put each issue so you can avoid being repetitive. This is why we at LawTutors love the outline. We absolutely cannot get enough of outlining, and we think it is the best thing ever. Well, at least when it comes to the bar exam!

(6) If you bring up something that may be of importance, like "independent contractor," be sure that you explain what it is, and what the standard or rule is. Here, we have neither, and have no clue why that status might be of importance. Also, it should be under Mary v. Clinic, not Mary v. Ben. Again, this is where an outline comes in handy. We know we are beating a dead horse, but for good reason. And not because we dislike horses.

(7) Why not discuss this further? He IS an employee—why is that important? Be sure to fully explain everything you bring up.

(8) Why is a discussion of 93(A) even relevant here? This is a perfect example of why it is necessary to spot the issues, and only discuss what is being asked. The bar examiners are looking to see if you will be a good attorney, and part of being a good attorney is spotting issues and knowing what to do with them. You don't bring a claim under 93(A) when you should be bringing a claim for medical malpractice.

General Comments

The lack of organization in this essay makes it difficult to read and understand. In addition, it fails to address important rules of law, or the application of such rules. We cannot stress enough how important it is to have an organized essay, but even more important is to lay out applicable rules of law and analyze them. Here, the author should have had something like, "Mary may have a claim of negligence against Ben. Ben had a duty, which was to act as a reasonable doctor would. Mary would have to prove that he breached that duty when he …".

The score is low on this essay because there is no application at all. Remember, the bar exam is not about what law you know, though that IS important, but how you APPLY the law you know.

SECURED TRANSACTIONS

Pat decided to purchase a laptop computer for her use in the kitchen and to bring on family trips with her children. On June 20, 2005, Pat went to Store, which specialized in computers, and asked for a recommendation for a lightweight and durable computer for home and travel use. The laptop computer (Laptop) recommended by Store cost more than Pat expected and Store's Manager asked Pat whether she wanted Store to finance the purchase. Pat agreed and Store loaned Pat $4,500 for the purchase of the Laptop. Pat signed Store's standard security agreement which described the Laptop and Pat left Store with the Laptop. Store did not file a financing statement.

Pat loved the Laptop and soon realized that it was far more efficient for her job as an independent sales consultant than her existing desktop. She started taking the Laptop to her office and used it almost exclusively for business purposes. She did not inform Store about this change of use. Pat's business grew and she obtained a $50,000 loan from Bank as operating capital, agreeing that Bank could have a security interest in all of her office equipment, including the Laptop she had purchased from Store. On October 1, 2005, Pat signed the security agreement Bank had requested and prepared and Bank duly filed a valid financing statement.

Pat defaulted on both her loan from Store and from Bank. On April 1, 2006, Store repossessed the Laptop. Both Store and Bank claim a security interest in the Laptop.

What are the rights of the parties?

Actual Bar Exam Answer To Question 18

Score = 1

In order to determine the rights of the parties here, a careful analysis of the facts in light of Massachusetts contract, UCC article 3 and secured transaction law is required.

When Pat went to the store and asked for a recommendation for a laptop and then bought the laptop, she was undertaking and entering into a contract to buy a good for over $500, she was entering into a UCC contract under article 3 for a negotiable instrument.**(1)** By entering into a financing agreement with the store, she had undertaken a secured transaction. The negotiable instrument was arguably not properly entered into since even though, there was a writing, the store's security agreement, it was not signed by both parties and the financing statement was not filed and would have made it legitimate as an enforceable instrument. **(2)** In a 2 party transaction, a payer pays the payee for the money and agreement entered into the purchase the property. **(3)** The transaction also arguably was simply a unilateral contract since the store did not provide any consideration **(4)** for the laptop and the transaction was for a good to be used in the home and not a business purpose. **(5)** By not informing the store of the change in use, Pat may have opened herself up to liability since she may not be accused of commiting her and misrepresentation of her personal and business expenses. The interest in the laptop was held by the store since in Massachusetts, a lien theory state, the store (mortgager) held title in the laptop until the $4500 approx had been paid off. **(6)**

Then, by attaching the laptop as a security interest when applying and thus getting the $50,000 loan, Pat was offering an interest she did not have as collateral. **(7)** Yet, since the laptop had not been properly formed, due to the lack of filing,**(8)** the Bank is likely to get the laptop and have first right to it in the repossession /foreclosure proceedings. Since Mass is a race-notice jurisdiction, by recording the financing statement 1st the Bank got 1st right to the laptop. Another key **(9)** is that by not informing the store of the "change in use" **(10)** they were not of notice of the laptop's purposes/uses which makes it a race to record. Even in a notice jurisdiction, the Bank would become the holder in due course of the laptop since when there is no notice knowledge by either party, the last conveyance wins, which would mean the bank wins.

Your Comments

(1) ____

____

____

(2) ____

____

____

(3) ____

____

____

(4) ____

____

____

(5) ____

____

____

(6) ____

____

____

(7) ____

____

____

(8) ____

____

____

(9) ____

____

____

(10) ____

____

____

Our Analysis

(1) This seems to be a very confused application. A sale of goods falls under UCC Article 2, while a transaction over $500 falls under the statute of frauds. In addition, Article 3 applies to negotiable instruments. There is also redundancy, as the author refers to a contract formed and then to entering into a UCC contract. To clarify the law, you enter into a contract, and it may be governed by the UCC. In addition, time and space is limited, so, as we've said before, avoid any redundancies. (It's okay for US to be redundant because we are teaching, but YOU cannot be redundant when you have limited time.)

(2) Yet again, this confuses various standards and does not lay out a clear standard for anything. Unlike the last essay, there is plenty of analysis here, but you still need the rule. Never put in one without the other!

(3) Grammar is very important. We realize that this is not a grammar exam, but the bar examiners have to understand the information you are conveying. In addition, poor grammar and sentence structure do not reflect well on your abilities as a potential attorney, so strive to write to the best of your ability. This has all been stated before, but we hope you are seeing a pattern with the low-scoring essays.

(4) There is consideration, and furthermore, the issue is the secured transaction, not contract formation. While it is always important to go through every necessary step, it is also important to sometimes assume facts, especially if they are given to you by the bar examiners. Plus, there is no issue as to whether there is consideration, as payment for something is the most traditional type of consideration.

(5) For purposes of this question, it does not matter if she told the store of her intended purpose. It might matter if she was bringing a claim for implied warranty of fitness for a particular purpose, but that is not at issue here.

(6) This seems to come out of nowhere. Why are mortgages brought into the essay? Remember to stick to the relevant topics, as your time is very limited. The time you spend outlining the topic helps to avoid putting in irrelevant law, such as this.

(7) It's unclear why the author thinks that the buyer has no collateral. The author may not be interpreting the facts correctly, but this shows why it is important to explain your thought process to the bar examiners.

(8) A security interest in a consumer product is automatically perfected and need not be filed. Obviously, there may be times where you pick the wrong rule of law to apply, or flat out get the rule wrong. Although not ideal, if you minimize the rest of the mistakes, it is less noticeable.

(9) "Key" what? Again, this is where grammar is important, so the examiners can easily comprehend what you are saying

(10) Pat was under no obligation to inform the store of change in use.

General Comments

In general, this essay seems to be all over the place and is very disorganized. It seems the author knew very little about the topic, or what he or she should write. This may happen on your exam. If it does, attempt to keep a clear head and strive to keep your essay coherent and on topic, even if you are unsure of what you are writing. This is where outlining comes in handy, as it helps you think about what you are going to write before you write it. Remember, you may be shaky on the law, but at least apply the principles you do know in an organized manner and use the methods you learn in this book for even the toughest of essays. The key is to not get shaken up and to try your best to maximize your points, even if the most you can score is a 3 due to not truly understanding the law well enough. Remember, a 3 is still better than a 1 and can make the difference between a passing and failing score.

EVIDENCE

Plaintiff sued Defendant in the Massachusetts Superior Court for personal injuries suffered as the result of Defendant's negligence when Defendant struck Plaintiff, a pedestrian, with his car. Defendant raised the affirmative defense of comparative negligence. At trial, the following evidence offered by Plaintiff and by Defendant was ruled admissible by the trial judge over objection.

In each instance, was the trial judge's ruling correct?

(a) By Plaintiff: The written report prepared by Doctor, Plaintiff's treating physician who died prior to trial. Doctor's report contained the following notations:
   (1) "Plaintiff states that he was struck by a car driven at a high rate of speed."
   (2) "In my opinion, Plaintiff will have permanent disabilities as a result of his injuries."

(b) By Plaintiff: The testimony of Plaintiff's wife, that Defendant had visited her after the accident and had made the following statements to her:
   (1) "I am so sorry for all the pain and suffering Plaintiff is going through from the accident."
   (2) "I'd like to help out with Plaintiff's medical bills."

(c) By Plaintiff: A copy of Defendant's automobile liability insurance policy, which had been provided to Plaintiff during pretrial discovery.

(d) By Defendant: The official police report prepared by the officer who investigated the accident, a portion of which contained the following statement made to the officer by Ike, an eyewitness to the accident: "I saw Plaintiff run out into the road in front of Defendant's car, and Defendant had no time to stop."

(e) By Defendant: The testimony of a witness, Wilson, that he had seen Plaintiff minutes before the accident and that in his opinion Plaintiff was drunk at that time.

(f) By Plaintiff: The testimony of Employer, Wilson's former employer and a resident of the town where Wilson lived, that (1) she had caught Wilson stealing from her and had fired him; and (2) in her opinion, Wilson was a dishonest person who could not be trusted to tell the truth.

Actual Bar Exam Answer To Question 19

Score = 1

(a)(1) If this was a statement that Plaintiff made for treatment under the professional care of the doctor, then it may be admissible if it falls under the business records exception.

Yet, under the business records exception the court should likely determine that this is hearsay under no recognized exception. **(1)**

(a)(2) Yes, judge made a correct ruling by allowing in Doctor's opinion on Plaintiff's condition after the accident. The court will have to determine that this evidence is relevant, and each of the other pieces of evidence in the problem are relevant. Relevant evidence is evidence that makes a material fact more probable or less probable than it would be without the evidence. **(2)**

(b)(1) Yes, trial judge's ruling was correct, because statements and admissions made while offering to pay for medical bills are admissible. **(3)**

(b)(2) No, statements offering to pay for medical bills are not admissible. This is based on public policy reasoning, since the courts are trying to encourage this type of action.

(c) Liability insurance can not be offered to prove negligence or ability to pay. However, it can be admitted to prove motive or bias to impeach the witness. It may also be used to show ownership and control. Thus, it depends on the reasoning behind the judge's ruling as to whether is should be upheld. **(4)**

(d) No, the judge's ruling was not correct. Even though the officer may make the police reports in the ordinary course of business, the witnesses statement is hearsay and thus the entire report cannot be allowed in. **(5)**

(e) The judge's ruling will likely be upheld if the reviewing court determines that the lay persons testimony is helpful to the trier of fact and the probative value of it is not outweighed by harm to the defendant. **(6)**

(f)(1) The Plaintiff is trying to show the truth or veracity or lack there of the witness, through a prior bad act. A witness may provide a witnesses prior convictions, or misdemeanors in MA. Yet, in this case, Wilson wasn't convicted of a felony or misdemeanor. Therefore, judge should not have allowed this prior bad act in through specific instances being recalled by witness.

(f)(2) No, employer may not offer her personal opinion concerning Wilson's truth or veracity.

Your Comments:

(1) ____

____

____

(2) ____

____

____

(3) ____

____

____

(4) ____

____

____

(5) ____

____

____

(6) ____

____

____

Our Analysis

(1) This is contradictory: does it come in or does it not? The law is also wrong and combines statements made for the purposes of medical diagnosis with the business records exception. There is also no explanation here as to why it may or may not come in. Remember, as we have stated in reviewing just about every essay, the analysis is the MOST important part, so even when pressed for time, do not leave it out.

Relevance is not the only hurdle evidence must overcome; make sure your evidence can jump through all the hoops before you allow it in. Also, the writer states the rule but yet again, leaves out any type of analysis.

(2) Is this always true? Be careful of blanket statements. In addition, you still need to give the bar examiners a rule and apply that rule. Notice that this directly contradicts the statement the writer makes immediately after. As we have already told you, contradictions are not the best way to showcase your legal knowledge.

(3) Avoid being vague: the examiners are giving you facts and they want you to apply them, not just state a rule and be done with it. The last sentence in this section should be struck entirely as unnecessary filler.

(4) WHY is it hearsay? As we have stated ad nauseam, if you give the bar examiners a rule, explain the rule and apply the facts. We know we are really repeating ourselves here, but an analysis is absolutely the most important part of your essay.

(5) Is that ALL that is needed? It just needs to be relevant and not be unduly prejudicial? What about the rules concerning lay opinions?

General Comments

Remember, there is always going to be a subject or two that may freak you out, but that does not mean you have to let the reader know that you are freaked out. Take a deep breath, realize this may not be your strongest subject, and maximize your points the best you can by using the methods we have taught and will continue to teach you throughout this book.

Do not just list rules—be sure to explain the rules and apply the facts. This essay has an alarming lack of facts, in addition to an alarming amount of wrong law. We listed in the six points what we found problematic about this essay, and we are sure you can find a lot more. We do not need to list everything that is wrong with this essay for you to understand that (1) the contradictory statements and lack of legal soundness and application resulted in the lowest score possible; and (2) even though the writer did answer all the questions, he or she only scored 1 point because none of the questions were answered using the system outlined for you at the beginning of this book.

General Note on Essays That Received 1s and 2s

As you can see, the essays that receive 1s and 2s are generally very disorganized, with very little rule application, or very few rules. You can avoid this by outlining and thinking about what you are going to write before you write it!

Conclusion

We really enjoyed writing this book. We know you already have the skills to pass the bar exam; we just wanted to find the most efficient and successful way for you to apply those skills. No matter what we have told you, we want to you rely on what you have seen in this book: actual graded bar exam answers. There is no better way to teach you how to write for the bar exam then to *show* you how it is done and what was achieved.

Now go out and pass the Massachusetts Bar Exam!